BEYOND
ALL YOU COULD ASK
OR THINK

BEYOND
ALL YOU COULD ASK
OR THINK

HOW TO PRAY LIKE THE APOSTLE PAUL

RAY PRITCHARD

MOODY PUBLISHERS
CHICAGO

All Scripture quotations, unless indicated, are taken from the *Holy Bible: New International Version.* NIV. Copyright © 1973, 1978, 1984 International Bible Society. Used by permission of Zondervan Publishing House. All rights reserved.

Scripture quotations marked KJV are from the King James Version.

Scripture quotations marked NLT are taken from the *Holy Bible, New Living Translation,* copyright © 1996. Used by permission of Tyndale House Publishers, Inc., Wheaton, Illinois 60189. All rights reserved.

Scripture quotations marked THE MESSAGE are from *The Message,* copyright © by Eugene H. Peterson 1993, 1994, 1995. Used by permission of NavPress Publishing Group.

Scripture quotations marked ESV are taken from *The Holy Bible, English Standard Version.* Copyright © 2000, 2001 by Crossway Bibles, a division of Good News Publishers. Used by permission. All rights reserved.

Scripture quotations marked AMP are taken from *The Amplified Bible.* Copyright © 1965, 1987 by The Zondervan Corporation. *The Amplified New Testament* copyright © 1958, 1987 by The Lockman Foundation. Used by permission.

Scripture quotations marked CEV are taken from the *Contemporary English Version.* Copyright © 1991, 1992, 1995 by American Bible Society. Used by permission.

Scripture quotations marked NEB are taken from the *The New English Bible.* Copyright © 1961 by Oxford University Press and Cambridge University Press. Used by permission.

Scripture quotations marked KNOX are taken from the *Holy Bible: A Translation from the Latin Vulgate in Light of the Hebrew and Greek Original.* Copyright © 1945, 1949. Used by permission.

The use of selected references from various versions of the Bible in this publication does not necessarily imply publisher endorsement of the versions in their entirety.

Library of Congress Cataloging-in-Publication Data

Pritchard, Ray, 1952-
      Beyond all you could ask or think : how to pray like the Apostle Paul
   / by Ray Pritchard.
         p. cm.
      Includes bibliographical references.
      ISBN 0-8024-3568-8
      1. Prayer. 2. Paul, the Apostle, Saint. I. Title.
   BV215.P77 2004
   248.3'2--dc22

                                                                2003025065

                         1 3 5 7 9 10 8 6 4 2

                   Printed in the United States of America

Contents

ACKNOWLEDGMENTS

Thank you to the many friends who have prayed for me. Kathy Duggins and Mia Gale helped greatly by proofing the sermons that these chapters were built upon. Special thanks to Greg Thornton, Bill Thrasher, and Ali Childers of Moody Publishers. Greg had the original vision that led to this book. These chapters were first presented as sermons to the congregation of Calvary Memorial Church in Oak Park, Illinois. Parts of these messages were shared with folks at Bible conferences at Word of Life Camp, in Schroon Lake, New York; at Living Waters Bible Camp, in Danforth, Maine; and at Gull Lake Bible and Missionary Conference, in Hickory Corners, Michigan. Prayer and fellowship with many godly people have strengthened my faith and joy. I am keenly aware that I could not have written this book without the love and support of my wife, Marlene, and our three sons—Joshua, Mark, and Nicholas.

INTRODUCTION

I didn't see the car until it was too late.

It happened like this. In the dead of winter, I decided to go for a bike ride. That's always a challenge if you live in the Chicago area, where winter can be treacherous, but I planned to go early in the afternoon while there was plenty of sunlight left. Things happened, my schedule got busy, and I didn't get around to my bike ride until almost 4:30 P.M. In the summer, that would mean there was plenty of daylight left; in January it meant that sundown was about forty minutes away. That was my first mistake. Since it was cold, I put on three or four layers of bulky clothing, then I pulled a thermal liner over my head and put a winter cap over the liner. That was my second mistake. Because it was late in the day, I ended up riding during rush hour, as thousands of tired motorists were making their way home. That was my third mistake. Part of my route took me along a very busy street. That was my fourth mistake. And I didn't put a light on my bike because I planned to be back before sundown. That was my fifth mistake.

I had just crossed a major thoroughfare and was heading toward an S curve. At the top of the S, there was an intersection, but I wasn't worried about it because you could only turn right, not left, which meant that any car on the other street would turn in the same direction I was going. However, cars often turned left (illegally) at that intersection. I know because I've seen it happen, and I've done it myself. But it was late in the afternoon, the sun was rapidly disappearing, the temperature was hovering in the low thirties, and the road was filled with shadows. I saw a car across the intersection, but I didn't worry about it because I assumed the driver would turn right. He didn't. He turned left, right into my path, ten feet away from me. There was no question about what was going to happen. He was about to hit me, and I couldn't do a thing about it.

In the movies, when a person is about to have an accident (or be shot), the action is slowed down so that person has time to review his whole life. I don't know if that really happens to people or not, but it didn't happen to me. I saw the car, knew it was going to hit me, and had time to do nothing but yell. Not a word or a phrase or a sentence, just a loud "Hey!" But it was too late. He never saw me. The car hit me broadside, which means the fender hit my leg and tossed me up in the air. Actually, I'm taking that by faith because it happened so fast that I don't remember anything except that one moment I was on my bike, and then I was lying on the hood of his car. Momentarily stunned, I looked up and saw his face through the windshield. He looked at me like I was a man from Mars. Maybe to him it was like one of those movie scenes where a man comes falling out of the sky and lands on your hood. He was so intent on quickly making his illegal left turn that he hadn't seen me in front of him.

And this is where the story takes an unusual turn. The front of the car hit me and knocked me off my bike onto the hood of his car. My bike landed in the middle of the busy street. It had all the makings of a disaster, but the disaster never happened. While lying on the hood, I started wiggling my arms and legs and the rest of my body. Everything seemed okay. I slid off the hood and picked up my bike, which also seemed unharmed. If there was any damage, it was to his car, but I couldn't even see a scratch. And, best of all, though it was a major street during rush hour, there was no traffic coming either way at that moment. I had escaped unscathed, unhurt, with not even a bruise. When I went over to the driver, all he could say was, "I never saw you." No kidding. So I told him I was okay, said, "God bless you," shook his hand, and off he went. Shaken from the wreck, I walked my bike home.

But that's not the end of the story. I told my wife about it that evening, and then I forgot about it by the next morning (which you tend to do when you have a close call but no injuries). But my wife told several people about it, and a friend came up to me later and reminded me of what I had said at the end of my sermon the day before the accident. Our church theme in 2003 was "Lord, Teach Us to Pray." At the end of my sermon on the first Sunday of the New Year, I did something I had never done before. I asked the congregation to earnestly pray for me during the coming year. I even asked them not to come into the sanctuary for the worship service without first praying for me. The earnestness of my appeal took even me by surprise, and several people later asked me why I asked for prayer now, at that moment in time. I did not have a clear answer to that question, but my friend did. She said, "You asked us to pray for you this year. That was on Sunday. The Lord knew you were going to have the accident on Monday. He intended to protect you, and that why He had you ask us to pray for you."

As I have thought about it, I am sure my friend is

correct. There is more to the story than simply protection from a bike accident that should have been much more. I believe the timing was not by accident. I believe God spared me through the prayers of others. None of us will know until we get to heaven how many times we were delivered from danger because someone prayed for us.

A FORGOTTEN SPIRITUAL TREASURY

If you want to learn how to pray, there are two main things you should do. First, you learn to pray by praying. That's the most basic step. Open your mouth and start talking to God. If you come in Jesus' name, with a sincere heart, He will not turn you away. Second, you learn to pray by listening to others as they pray. For new Christians, this may be the most important step of all. We tell new believers to get in a group and just listen as others pray. Soon you'll know how to pray yourself. You learn by doing and by listening. And one of the best ways to do this is to study the great prayers of the Bible. There are many prayers in the Bible, and each of them teaches us something important, but there is an overlooked treasury of spiritual truth close at hand—the prayers of the apostle Paul in his epistles. These are the prayers Paul included in his letters to the Philippians, the Colossians, the Ephesians, the Romans, and the Thessalonians.

This little book is a journey through some significant prayers that the great apostle prayed. Our goal is three-fold:

1. We want to know what Paul said when he prayed.
2. We want to know what God is saying to us through these ancient prayers.
3. We want our own prayers to become closer to these great Bible prayers of Paul.

Chapter by chapter we'll listen carefully to the prayers of one of the greatest Christians who ever lived. As we listen to his prayers, our own prayers will no doubt be changed. Many of us have lived too long in spiritual kindergarten when it comes to prayer. Some Christians never get beyond the "bless Aunt Bessie" level of prayer. When they pray, it's "Bless my children, bless my spouse, bless my friends, bless my church, bless the sick, bless the poor, bless the missionaries, and while you're at it, Lord, bless everyone everywhere." Now on one level, there is nothing wrong with this sort of prayer if it is offered in sincerity. The blessing of God is a wonderful thing, and we ought to ask God to bless others. But there is more to prayer than asking God to bless someone. The prayers of Paul will challenge us to go both broader and deeper when we pray for others.

PRAYING FOR OTHERS

For me, the challenge came early on. As I began to study the prayers of Paul, a massive truth hit home that I had never clearly seen before. In fact, so stunning was the revelation, it felt as if the Holy Spirit slapped me in the face. *God is greatly glorified when we pray for others.* I don't know why that had never hit me before, but it hadn't. I'm not sure I had ever thought about praying for others as a means of glorifying God. But I can think of at least five reasons why that is true.

God is glorified when we pray for others because:

1. We are responding to needs in a Christlike manner.
2. We are demonstrating that we believe God's Word about prayer is true.
3. One part of the body of Christ is moving to meet the needs of another part.
4. We are partnering with God to further His work in the world.
5. He gets the praise and glory when the answers come.

Sometimes (often, perhaps) we may view intercessory prayer as a burden or even a distraction from the "real work" of life. But nothing could be further from the truth. Our God is greatly honored when we take time to pray for others. By our prayers we help those for whom we pray, and we also bring glory to our heavenly Father. When the puny arm of man is linked to the mighty arm of God's omnipotence, miracles are let loose on the earth.

Through intercessory prayer we partner with God in helping those in need. The thought of partnering with God is an exciting concept. It means that when I am on my knees, I can make contact with the most powerful force in the universe. As I pray, my motives are purified, my faith is strengthened, and my heart is focused on eternal things. When I pray, I am in touch with Almighty God himself, the Creator of the heavens and the earth. *Through my halting words and my stumbling petitions, I join hands with God to bless others and to advance His cause in the world.* The Holy Spirit aids me in linking up with the heart of God when I do not know what to pray (Romans 8:26–27). By prayer I am knocking holes in the darkness and rolling back Satan's evil dominion. This is why "the devil trembles when he sees, the weakest saint upon his knees."

We experience heightened joy as we see our prayers being answered. This truth brings us face-to-face with a question thoughtful believers sometimes ask. Why does the church emphasize praying together? Isn't it just as effective for me to pray by myself? Why can't I pray while I ride my bike and you pray while you drive your car? The answer is, I can and you can, and we should, but that doesn't tell the whole story. There are at least two things that happen when we pray together that cannot happen when we pray alone. First, when we pray together, our faith is mutually strengthened. If we are in a small group, it is inevitable that some people will come with strong faith, others with weak faith, and others somewhere in-between. As we pray, the prayers of one person will spark something in another person and vice versa. And we all leave the prayer time with stronger faith than we had in the beginning. Second, when we pray together, the joy is multiplied when the answers finally come. We've all seen this happen, I'm sure. We may be praying for a loved one who is desperately ill and for whom the outlook seems hopeless. But when the doctor says, "I can't explain it, but she is much better today," word spreads and all those who prayed so long and so hard begin to laugh and cry and hug each other. Our rejoicing is louder and longer and more public when we have prayed together.

A PLACE TO BEGIN

I have several purposes in mind in writing this book. I hope to encourage you to pray more intentionally for other people. I suppose most of us pray for others from time to time, yet we are often stymied because we don't know what to say. The prayers of Paul help us at precisely that point. They give us models to follow.

Sometimes they will help us find the very words to say. And I hope to encourage you to pray more intentionally with other people. There is enormous power unleashed when believers come together to seek the Lord.

Each chapter of this book covers a single prayer by the apostle Paul. I haven't tried to cover every prayer Paul prayed. Instead, I have focused on those prayers that present different aspects of the Christian life. You will discover in this book a prayer for discernment (Chapter 1), a prayer for knowledge (Chapter 2), a prayer for enlightenment (Chapter 3), a prayer for power (Chapter 4), a prayer for endurance (Chapter 5), and a prayer for stability (Chapter 6). And, as you will discover, this little book is not a commentary on every aspect of these six prayers. My main goal in each chapter is to take each prayer, pick it up, shake it a little bit, and then turn it upside down and see what falls out first. The part that falls out first will always be the key thought of the prayer. Paul did not pray "random" prayers that wandered from here to there with no rhyme or reason. Certainly some of his longer prayers may seem that way, but a closer examination will always show that no matter how long or complex the prayer may be, Paul always had only one major thought in mind for each prayer. That is, he prayed for <u>one main thing and one main thing only</u> in Philippians 1. And that "one thing" was different from what he prayed in Colossians 1 or 2 Thessalonians 2.

My goal will be accomplished only if this book actually helps you pray more effectively. And that's why we'll focus on the key thought of each prayer. And that's also why we'll pass over some of the secondary details. Each chapter begins with the prayer as we find it in the New Testament. And each chapter ends with a rewording of the prayer in contemporary language to help you put Paul's words into your own words.

No matter where you are on your spiritual journey, the prayers of Paul will help you take another step in the right direction. They show us how to pray, and if we listen to them carefully, they also make us want to pray. That has been my experience, and I hope it will be yours as well.

NOTE TO
THE READER

There are several ways to read this book. The simplest way is to read it straight through—which won't take very long. But that's probably not the best way to learn the prayers of Paul. You'll get the greatest benefit from reading one chapter at a time and pondering its meaning. Since this is not a mystery novel, don't feel as if you have to hurry through it to find out how it ends. The prayers of Paul are more suited to a leisurely stroll than to a hundred-yard dash. Read a little bit, think about it, and then take time to pray. Feel free to underline the text and to jot down questions and personal insights in the margin. You may want to use it as part of your daily quiet time with the Lord or you might enjoy reading it as part of a small group Bible study or a Sunday school class. I think you'll probably grow faster if you study it with other Christians who are also committed to spiritual growth. As iron sharpens iron, your friends will have insights you missed, and you will discover truth they didn't see. As you listen to others pray, you will discover how the prayers of Paul can shape your own walk with God.

This is *your* book and I want it to help *you*. I have a friend who has taken the prayers of Paul and uses them every day as a guide to help him pray for others. He has printed them out and left blanks at certain points so he can insert the names of friends and loved ones. By doing this he has made Paul's prayers his own, and has found a way to pray effectively for others. At the end of each chapter, I have offered a contemporary version of each prayer. You might enjoy doing the same thing so that you end up with your own personal version of these ancient prayers.

No matter how you read this book, maximum impact will come chapter by chapter, prayer by prayer, as you ponder the way Paul prayed for others. As you will discover, Paul had the gift of packing enormous truth into just a few words. Where we might take a hundred words to say something, Paul could say it in less than a sentence. To take just one example, at one point Paul prays that his readers might "be filled to the measure of all the fullness of God" (Ephesians 3:19). You could easily spend a week, a month, a year, or a lifetime understanding and applying the meaning of those eleven words.

So the message is simple: Take your time as you read this book. Read it slowly, think about what it says, and then start making Paul's prayeers your own. The more time you take, the greater the impact will be in your own life.

PHILIPPIANS 1:9—11

✣

*"And this is my prayer: that your love may
abound more and more in knowledge and depth
of insight, so that you may be able to discern
what is best and may be pure and blameless
until the day of Christ, filled with the fruit of
righteousness that comes through Jesus Christ—
to the glory and praise of God."*

DON'T SETTLE
FOR SECOND BEST

How would you rate your prayer life? If you had to give yourself a grade, would it be an A, B, C, D, or F? Or would you choose the word "incomplete"? Before you decide on an answer, let's phrase the question another way. Is your prayer life A) Excellent, B) Above average, C) Average, D) Below average, or F) "I need big help!" Probably many of us would choose F simply because we feel our prayer life truly does need help.

As we think about prayer, let's begin with three simple statements:

1. *Prayer is both the easiest and hardest discipline of the Christian life.* It is the easiest in that the youngest child and the newest Christian can learn to pray. Even the slightest motion of the soul toward God is a form of genuine prayer. If a person says, "Lord, have mercy," he is truly praying. But prayer is also the hardest discipline. It is difficult to maintain a consistent prayer life. In a sense it is easy to enroll in the School of Prayer but hard to get a graduate degree.

2. *Almost everyone prays, believers and non-believers, and almost everyone feels he can improve in this area.* Even in our best moments, we still must admit that we have barely touched the hem of the Master's garment in the arena of prayer.

3. *Prayer presents us with both theological and practical problems.* On one level, we are faced with difficult questions regarding the sovereignty of God and human free will. While those questions are important, I am not going to address them in this chapter. I would rather tackle the challenge of prayer on a purely practical level. When we pray, what should we pray for? I am much more interested in the "what" and "how" of prayer that pertains to us every day.

"Prayer is the very sword of the saints," said Francis Thompson. If that is true, why do we often keep the sword in the scabbard? Lee Roberson called prayer "the Christian's secret weapon, forged in the realms of glory." Why, then, do we not use it more effectively? *Often we simply don't know what to say when we pray.* I'm thinking especially of those moments when we begin to pray for others beyond our most intimate circle. What do you do when you have a large list of people to pray for, including friends, loved ones, neighbors, co-workers, missionaries, and others whom you hardly know at all? Our usual response is to pray like this: "Lord, uh . . . uh . . . uh . . . bless Sally." Then we go to the next name: "And . . . uh . . . please bless Bill." Then we go to the next name: "Uh . . . Lord, I ask You to really bless our missionaries in Ghana." And on it goes. As one man remarked, if you took the word "bless" out of our prayer vocabularies, some of us would never pray again. While I believe it is perfectly appropriate to ask God to bless people, I think we can move far beyond that and, in so doing, dramatically increase the effectiveness of our prayers. We can use Paul's prayers for the Philippians as blueprints for powerful praying. Philippians 1:9–11 is a prayer that fits virtually every situation we may face. If we understand the meaning of Paul's words, we can truly pray for anyone about anything.

This is a case where we do not have to wonder

about the theme of Paul's prayer. It is spelled out for us in verse 10. The heart of his prayer is his request **"that you may be able to discern what is best."** This is a prayer for spiritual discernment. Here's my version of Paul's prayer:

> *I pray that you will know:*
> *The good from the bad,*
> *The better from the good, and*
> *The best from the better.*

As I thought about this request, my mind drifted to the motto of the public high school in the village where I live. If you look at the school's Web site, it contains a shield with a Greek word written across it. The word is *tagarista,* which means "those things that are best." It's a noble goal—both for a high school and for an individual's life—to pursue *tagarista.* The people who proposed this motto for the high school understood that there is a moral dimension to all education. That is, the very notion that there is "the best" presupposes a better, a good, a not-so-good, and a definitely bad. You can hardly choose "those things that are best" unless you know what they are, and you cannot know what they are unless you know what is "the best." This means that education in its truest sense is more than the impartation of facts about geometry, biology,

American history, or English literature. It is also an understanding of a moral framework that enables us to make proper judgments about the good, the better, and the best (not to mention the bad, the very bad, and the worst). But apart from God, how will we know the good from the bad, the better from the good, and the best from the better? The answer is, we won't. Education alone will never lead us to *tagarista*. Education gives us knowledge, but to choose those things that are best, we need the wisdom that comes from God, and that's why Paul prayed this prayer.

THREE REQUESTS

Paul's prayer begins with three requests for the Philippian believers. As we pray for others, we should feel perfectly free to include these three requests as our own.

1. Abounding Love

"And this is my prayer: that your love may abound more and more" (Philippians 1:9a). Imagine an empty cup slowly being filled with water. When the water reaches the brim, it begins to overflow down the sides of the cup. That's the picture Paul has in mind—love filling the hearts of the Philippians until it overflows. Almost all of Paul's prayers in the New Testament begin with a petition for love. That's because love is supreme among the Christian virtues. It alone will last forever (1 Corinthians 13:8, 13). No matter how much love we have, our love can always increase. He is praying that they would love more people and would love them in a greater way. We might ask if Paul is thinking about (1) love for God, (2) love for fellow Christians, and/or (3) love for non-Christians. The answer of course is yes, all of the above. The text is not specific because our love for God is always tied to our love for other people. If a man says he loves God and hates his brother, he is a liar (1 John 4:20). *Love is the supreme grace. You can never have too much of it. You can never have enough of it.* Paul is saying, "I pray that God will make you an overflowing fountain of love." He is praying that they might become "Super Lovers." There is an amazing scene at the end of the movie *Marvin's Room.*[1] Bessie, played by Diane Keaton, has cared for her ill father and her aunt for twenty years. After learning that she has leukemia, Bessie receives a visit from her estranged sister, Lee, played by Meryl Streep. Bessie tells Lee, "I've been lucky to have had so much love in my life." Lee agrees that their father and aunt really do love her. Bessie seems taken aback for a moment. Her sister doesn't understand. Bessie doesn't mean she's lucky to be loved; she means she is lucky to have had so much love to give to others.

Lucky to love. What an amazing perspective. If we

are full of God's love, it will overflow to others. It's not enough to be kind and polite. Our love must constantly be growing. So I ask a question at this point: Why does Paul pray for overflowing love? The answer is that *when hard times come, we naturally start to pull away from other people and start focusing on our own problems. Sometimes Christian love is the first casualty of hard times.* It's so easy to become self-centered, demanding, and myopic. If our marriage is in trouble, that's all we talk about. If our children are not doing well, that's all we talk about. If we have health problems, that's all we talk about. If we have lost a job, that's all we talk about. It's all about us, our problems, our struggles, and our hardships. We hardly have time or energy for anything else. And sometimes our distress is so great that we become vicious, turning on those we love the most. But it doesn't have to be that way. Some people build walls through their trials that keep people an arm's length away. Others build bridges so they can connect with and serve God's people. I received a wonderful note from a friend who wrote:

> "Life is *so* good with God in the center. Now problems turn into solutions, fear turns into hope, anger turns to love. I'm free in God, and it's the *best* place to be. I've learned to take risks and face challenges. I take no credit for any of this. To God be all the glory. He never let go. He took me from a

bitter, unhappy, depressed alcoholic and gave me the wings of eagles, soaring to heights I never dreamed possible. He's given me his words to share with other alcoholics, restored my family, and filled me with his love each day."

That testimony is wonderful in many respects, not least because it perfectly illustrates what it means to have love overflowing in your life. Only God can do that, and He does it wherever He can find a willing heart.

It's easy to understand why Paul's prayer begins with love. Since we live in a fallen world, we often find ourselves surrounded by irritable, petulant, cranky, annoying, aggravating, frustrating, crabby, unreasonable, and cantankerous people. And that's on a good day! Sometimes people will do or say foolish things to deliberately irritate us. And let's face it—some people are just very hard to love. What do we do then? There are many answers to that question, but our text suggests one very practical answer: We should pray for our love to increase.

It's one thing to pray, "Lord, get this fool away from me before I say something I shouldn't," and it's another thing to pray, "Lord, please change this person so he won't be so obnoxious." But it's something else entirely to pray, "Lord, I really don't care for this person. I don't like this person. He gets on my nerves. He's a total jerk. He's a bossy, dominating, opinionated fool.

I don't even want to love him or like him, and I prefer not to be around him at all. I now ask you to bypass my feelings and do whatever it takes to increase my love. I'm low on love, Lord, and I ask You to fill me up." That's a prayer God will be glad to answer. By the way, I'm in favor of honest prayer. Why not be straightforward with God about the way we feel? David poured out his soul to the Lord and in the process used colorful language to describe his enemies. God knows how you feel anyway. It's not as if when you say that you can't stand someone the Lord says, "I'm surprised to hear that. I thought you liked them."

On more than one occasion I have poured out my frustrations about people to the Lord and then said, "Lord, You know how I feel. I now ask You to overlook all that I've said and bless the person anyway." And then, "Lord, do a work of healing in my heart so that I can love as I ought." Love is the glue that holds the human race together. It enables us to overlook the faults of others while acknowledging that we ourselves are far from perfect.

Growing Knowledge

"In knowledge and depth of insight" (Philippians 1:9b). Paul's prayer continues with a request that the Philippians might grow in their knowledge of God. This sort of knowledge goes beyond factual information. It is a kind of knowing that comes from a deep, personal, and intimate relationship with another person. In context, Paul is asking that their love express itself in an intimate knowledge of who God is. The Greek word for "insight" speaks of moral discrimination, the ability to look at various options and to say, "This one is good. That's not so good. This one is better. That one is best."

Sometimes we say, "Love is blind." On the contrary, God says, "Love needs clear vision." Our love needs the guidance of knowledge and deep insight or else we will end up loving things we ought not to love —and entering into relationships that are not good for us. While love is supreme, it is never enough.

> Not every relationship is a good relationship.
>
> Not every choice is a good choice.
>
> Not every friendship is good for us.
>
> Not every job is a wise career move.
>
> Not every roommate is a healthy choice.
>
> Not every purchase is a wise use of our money.

We make our choices, and then our choices turn around and make us. As a tiny rudder guides a massive ship, our lives often turn on small decisions and unexpected events. An unplanned phone call, a chance conversation in the hallway, a friend we "happened" to meet in a restaurant, a fragment of a remembered dream, a book we meant to return but didn't, the dry cleaning we forgot to pick up, a newspaper story that led to an idea that became a dissertation topic that earned a degree that opened a door to a job in another country. It happens all the time. Every day we make hundreds of decisions, most of them made either by habit or on the spur of the moment.

> Will I get up in the morning?
> Will I take a shower?
> Will I eat breakfast?
> Will I go to work today?
> If so, will I take the car or ride the train?
> If I take the car, will I listen to the radio or a CD?
> If I ride the train, what will I read while I'm on the train?
> Who will I greet first at work?
> Who will I see before first period starts at school?
> Who will I meet for lunch?
> What will we talk about?
> What will do I when I get home?
> What e-mails will I answer?
> What Internet sites will I visit?
> What books will I read?
> How will I respond to my spouse?
> How much time will I spend with my children?

On and on the questions go. Hundreds of questions, one after another, little decisions made on the fly every day. We like to think those decisions don't matter, but they do because each decision is connected to every other decision, like so many links in the chain of life itself. In a profound sense you are the sum total of all the choices you have made stretching back to your childhood. Each little decision joins you to the past and leads inexorably into the future. Choices aren't "neutral," since each one either leads us toward the light of God or toward the darkness of despair. Some things that don't seem to matter today may be of enormous consequence tomorrow, and some things that keep us awake for hours will prove to be relatively unimportant. We need "insight" from God to make wise choices. Here's a good way to remember the concept of insight. It is "sight" on the inside, a kind of inner vision that enables us to properly evaluate all the choices we face every day. When we have it, we make good decisions. And when we don't have it, we end up making the same dumb mistakes over and over again.

Where do we find this kind of insight? First, *we get insight from the Word of God with the aid of the Holy Spirit.* As we study the Bible, the Holy Spirit takes the Word of God and reveals to us the things of God (1 Corinthians 2:6–16). Let a man dive into the Scriptures with an open heart, and very soon his whole life will begin to change. In essence, Paul wants the Philippians to learn to think "Christianly" in every situation. Second, *we get insight from the Lord in the answers to our prayers.* So if you are confused, or if you find yourself in a deep hole because of wrong choices made over and over again, humbly ask God for the insight to make the right choices in life. That leads directly to the third petition, which is the heart of the prayer.

Increasing Discernment

"So that you may be able to discern what is best" (Philippians 1:10a). Eugene Peterson (THE MESSAGE) offers this colorful paraphrase, "You need to use your head and test your feelings so that your love is sincere and intelligent, not sentimental gush." KNOX translates this way: "that you may learn to prize what is of value." The NEB speaks of the "gift of true discrimination." The NLT offers this translation: "I want you to understand what really matters." The Greek word for "discern" was used to describe the process of testing metals, such as gold ore and coins, to find out what they were worth. There is gold, and then there is "fool's gold." It looks like gold to the naked eye, but it isn't, and it's not worth anything. Too many Christians settle for "fool's gold" in the choices they make.

Paul prays that the Philippians would have such love and insight that they would continually make wise choices in life. He is praying that they would not be satisfied with the status quo or with spiritual mediocrity but would push on to true spiritual excellence. In a sense he is asking God for the gift of spiritual discrimination. In our day the word "discrimination" has a mostly negative tone, but in the spiritual realm we desperately need to discriminate between good and bad, good and better, better and best. This kind of discrimination is the ability to make wise choices under pressure. God's people need to learn discernment so that they can make wise choices under pressure.

Parents with young children understand this principle. As children grow up, we will correct them by saying, "The choice that you made was not good." Last Friday night my wife and I sat in the stands watching a high school football game. At one point one of the players from our local high school committed a foul, and the referee threw his flag. Marlene turned to me and said, "He didn't make a good choice."

"No, he didn't," I replied. "He hit the ball carrier after the whistle blew."

This is an important prayer request for parents to offer on behalf of their children. Pray that your children (and your grandchildren) learn to make wise choices under pressure. This is crucial because most of us can make wise choices if we have two days to think about it. But life usually doesn't work that way, especially for the young. They have to make split-second decisions every day about what they will wear, where they will go, who they will go with, what jokes they will tell, what music they will listen to, what movies they will watch, and whether or not they will stand up for their faith. Young people today are on the firing line all the time. Pray for your children that they will have wisdom from God to choose what is best when they don't have much time to make up their minds.

There are really two parts to making wise choices: First, you must know what is right. We live in a world where many people have lost all sense of right and wrong. Everything appears to them as shades of gray. Second, you must have the courage to choose what you know to be right. I happened to catch a few minutes of a televised speech by Supreme Court Justice Clarence Thomas. During the question time someone asked how he managed to deal with all the criticism that comes to anyone in a high-profile position. He replied that the most important thing in life is to discover what you believe to be true and then to stand up for those beliefs no matter what. He then added these words: "If you do what you know is right, it doesn't matter what people think." True discernment gives you vision to see what is right and then the courage to choose to do it.

THREE RESULTS

Paul's prayer continues with the results that flow from the three requests just mentioned—love, knowledge, and discernment.

A Blameless Life

"And may be pure and blameless until the day of Christ" (Philippians 1:10b). Note two key words in this phrase. The word "pure" comes from two other words that mean "judgment" and "sunlight." In the first century the shops were often dimly lit, which meant that prospective customers would have trouble viewing the wares. When they took the pottery or the fabric into the sunlight, they could see it as it really was. The sunlight revealed the truth and allowed the customer to make a proper judgment. You can't determine the value of an object until you can see it clearly. *To be pure means to live in such a way that the truth about who you are is clear.* It means that people don't have to wonder about what you are doing in the darkness because you have nothing to hide. To be "pure" means to be a "sunlight" Christian. Your life is consistent no matter where you happen to be or who happens to be with you.

You are the same in the darkness as you are in the light.

You are the same at midnight as you are at high noon.

You are the same on the job, or at school, as you are in church on Sunday morning.

You are the same behind closed doors as you are in public.

In Greek, the word "blameless" derives from a word with an opposite meaning. This word, "scandal," originally referred to the bait in a trap that would catch unsuspecting animals. It came to mean a lifestyle that caused others to fall into sin. In contrast, a "blameless" person is free from moral scandal. You don't stumble into sin, and you don't cause others to stumble by your behavior.

To be pure and blameless means to be "above reproach," which is a quality demanded of spiritual leaders (1 Timothy 3:2). Leaders' words, motives, and actions are questioned and criticized. A leader who is truly above reproach weathers the storm because there is nothing about him which a person could say, "Aha! Gotcha." This means no questionable conduct, no secret sins, and no deliberately unresolved conflicts. The word "integrity" sums it up well. A man or woman with integrity has nothing hidden because there is nothing to hide.

Several years ago my older brother took me to visit a cemetery outside Florence, Alabama, near the remains of a mansion called Forks of Cypress. James Jackson, an early settler of northwest Alabama, built it in the 1820s. My brother and I walked among the ruins of the mansion and then crossed the country road into the dense forest on the other side. After about a quarter-mile we found the Jackson family cemetery. There was no sign marking the spot, only a five-foot-high stone wall surrounding about fifty graves. Inside we found a tall marker over James Jackson's grave with a long inscription extolling his virtues, which were many.

As I walked along, my gaze locked on the marker for one of his sons. There was a name, a date of birth, and a date of death, and this simple five-word epitaph: "A man of unquestioned integrity."

Five words to sum up an entire life. Sixty-plus years distilled into five words. But, oh, what truth they tell.

"A man of unquestioned integrity." I cannot think of a better tribute.

A Fruitful Life

"Filled with the fruit of righteousness that comes through Jesus Christ" (Philippians 1:11a). The Bible often uses the metaphor of a fruit tree to describe both the life of the righteous and the life of the wicked. Regarding false prophets, Jesus declared that by their fruit we would know them (Matthew 7:20). That's precisely what Paul is praying for—the fruit of visible Christian character. *A fruitful life is one that is distinctively Chris-*

tian in every aspect. It reminds me of the question, "If you were arrested for being a Christian, would there be enough evidence to convict you?" The fruitful life can always answer "yes."

Note that this fruit comes "through Jesus Christ." As we are rooted deeply in Him, and as we draw our strength from Him, His power flows through us and produces the "fruit of righteousness" in us. He is the root, and His power produces the fruit.

A Theo-Doxic Life

"To the glory and praise of God" (Philippians 1:11b). Don't look for the word "theo-doxic" in your dictionary, because I made it up. "Theo" means "God" and "doxic" means "glory" (as in the word "doxology"). *A "theo-doxic" life is one that brings glory or praise to God.* Such a person actually magnifies God's reputation in the world.

When people see you, do they naturally think about God? Does your life serve as a good advertisement for the Lord Jesus Christ? I grew up in a small town in Alabama where my father was a well-known and well-loved surgeon. I was one of four sons—Andy, Ray, Alan, and Ron. Often I was introduced with these words: "This is one of Dr. Pritchard's sons." Because I bore my father's name, I knew I had an obligation not to ruin his name by the way I lived—and to bring honor to him if I could. My father died thirty years ago, and I still miss him today. With the passing of each year, there are fewer and fewer people who knew my father. And since I live hundreds of miles from where I grew up, I rarely meet anyone who knew him. But the length of time that he has been gone does not in any way lessen the sacred responsibility I have to honor his name—to live up to the things he taught me, to try to be as good a man as he was, and to live in such a way so that people who never knew him will look at me and say, "His father must have been a good man," and the people who knew my dad will say, "Your father would be proud of you."

But that is not the only name I bear. As a child of God, I bear the name of my heavenly Father. Honoring His name means living in such a way that I help more people to know Him. When I've done it well, people who don't know God will look at my life and say, "He must have a great God" and God will look down from heaven with a smile and say, "That's my boy!"

Have you ever heard Ruth Bell Graham's definition of a saint? *A saint is a person who makes it easy to believe in Jesus.* When we live for "the glory and praise of God," we'll be saints who make it easy for others to believe in Jesus.

Before we finish, let's step back and consider how great this prayer is. One nineteenth-century writer called it "The Life of God in the Soul of Man." In some ways that phrase summarizes all that God wants to do in us and through us:

1. It starts with abounding love,
2. That manifests itself in knowledge and discernment,
3. Resulting in the ability to make wise choices under pressure,
4. Producing the visible fruit of a righteous life,
5. That comes from a living relationship with Jesus Christ,
6. So that God alone gets the glory.

Who are you praying for today? *Remember that prayer is not a ritual but a matter of the heart.* To pray for someone else is an act of hidden kindness that only God sees. And because God alone sees your heart, He will hear your prayer and reward you in secret. We can touch people through prayer that we couldn't touch any other way. Prayer is the secret sword of the saints. Use it! God gave you a secret weapon so that by your prayer you can change the world.

When you boil it all down to the essentials, Paul prayed for *tagarista*. He prayed that the Philippians would have the wisdom to choose the best things in life. And he didn't mean "the best things" in general; he meant God's best for them. This is an inspiring thought and a good way to organize our prayers.

Do you want God's best for others?

Pray this prayer!

Do you want God's best in your own life?

Pray this prayer!

Do you want God's best in your family?

Pray this prayer!

Do you want God's best in your church?

Pray this prayer!

May God deliver us from second-best Christianity!

May God deliver us from spiritual mediocrity!

Lord Jesus, grant that my love may overflow so that I will love the irritating people I meet. I pray for insight to see beyond the external and the immediate to see what really matters so that I can make wise choices under pressure. Make me a "sunlight" Christian who makes it easy for others to believe in You. May my life bring glory to Your name.

Amen.

COLOSSIANS 1:9—14

✦

*"For this reason, since the day we heard about you,
we have not stopped praying for you and asking
God to fill you with the knowledge of his will
through all spiritual wisdom and understanding.
And we pray this in order that you may live a life
worthy of the Lord and may please him in every
way: bearing fruit in every good work, growing in
the knowledge of God, being strengthened with all
power according to his glorious might so that you
may have great endurance and patience, and joyfully giving thanks to the Father, who has quali-
fied you to share in the inheritance of the saints in
the kingdom of light. For he has rescued us from
the dominion of darkness and brought us into the
kingdom of the Son he loves, in whom we have redemption, the forgiveness of sins."*

2

How to Pray with Power

This particular prayer by the apostle Paul contains 143 words in the *New International Version.* In the King James Version, it comes in at 132 words. In the *New Living Translation,* 171 words. And in the *Amplified Bible,* a whopping 223 words. A friend who had the Greek text counted 109 words—but Greek is an efficient language. Like several of his other prayers, it is one long sentence in Greek—filled with participles, infinitives, and clauses that seem to pile on top of each other. Even though the NIV breaks it down into three sentences, that doesn't help very much. Paul packed a lot into these six verses. If you read it out loud, the whole prayer takes about a minute to read. I'm sure that this is a *Reader's Digest* version in which Paul gives us a summary of what was probably a much longer prayer. You could take any phrase in this prayer and form a prayer around it. It is dense with spiritual truth.

I want to make sure we don't get lost in the details and miss the main point. Here is a simple outline of the prayer: It contains one request, one purpose, and four results.

THE REQUEST

Paul has only one basic request in mind. You can find it in verse 9 if you lift out the key phrase and hold it up for close inspection. He is **"asking God to fill you with the knowledge of his will."** That little phrase is the heart and soul of this prayer. Paul prays that the Colossians will know the will of God for their lives. He asks God to give them wisdom and spiritual insight so that they will know God's will. That's a very practical prayer, if you think about it. *Almost everyone I know thinks about the will of God at one time or another.* We tend to wonder about God's will when it comes to the major decisions of life: knowing where to go to college, searching for the right job, deciding whether or not to get married, choosing a church, buying a new home, moving to a new location, going to the mission field, investing money, having children, and so on. Wanting to know the will of God in those circumstances is a legitimate desire, but Paul seems to have something bigger and deeper and broader in mind when he uses this phrase. I think the key is the word "fill," which means in Greek to be filled to overflowing. It can also mean "engulfed" or "overwhelmed" by something. It has the idea of "fully possessing" or "controlling" or "becoming the dominating influence." If a person is frightened, we say he is "filled with fear." If he speaks harshly, we say he is "filled with anger." If he is generous to all he meets, he is "filled with kindness." So what does that concept mean in this verse?

If you are filled with the knowledge of God's will, then you will want what God wants for your life. In many ways, this is a very challenging standard. Often we pray "Your will be done" without ever considering what those words really mean. Too often we mean something like this: "O Lord, show me Your will so I can carefully consider it to see if it fits into my plans." But that's a prayer God will never answer because He does not offer His will for you to consider it, as if it were an invitation to have lunch next Thursday if you happen to be free and if you don't get a better offer. To truly say "Your will be done in my life" means something like this:

> *Lord, let Your will be done in me whatever it costs,*
> *whatever it takes, wherever it leads.*

Let Your will be done even if
it means that my will is not done.
Let Your plans go forward even if
it means changing my plans.

To say it that way implies a huge spiritual truth that we can express in a simple syllogism:

God has a will (or desire) for your life.
But you also have a will (or desire) for your life.
When you pray, "Your will be done," you are asking that His will take precedence over your will.

Only one will can be done at a time. *Either God calls the shots, or you call the shots.* Either He is in control, or you are in control. Praying for God's will to be done may seem hard since it means giving up control of your own life. But you aren't really in control anyway. It only seems that way.

"I'm going to relax now."

Several years ago I had lunch with a man who was rising to the top of his profession. I do not know his salary, but I am sure he is well compensated for his labors. But his outward prosperity is only part of the story. He has known his share of pain and sorrow.

Tragedy has struck close to home once and then twice. He is outgoing and friendly, and you feel drawn to him immediately. However, if you look deeply in his eyes, you can see the evidence of the burdens he has carried.

When we ate lunch, he was in the middle of great turmoil at his job. Every day he faced the reality of going to work knowing that his superiors did not appreciate his contributions to the firm. This was true even though he was far and away the top producer and the star performer. His labors brought enormous profit to the company. Every day was a battle to get up, go to work, and keep a smile on his face. But he looked so relaxed when I ate lunch with him. How did he do it? He told me that a great change had come to his life in the last few days. It was a change on the inside, a change in the way he looked at things. "Pastor, I've been pushing and pushing and pushing. Trying to fix things up. Trying to make a better deal. Holding all my cards, dealing them out one by one. It hasn't worked. The Lord finally said to me, 'Why don't you let Me take over?' So I did. I told the Lord that He could take over. Nothing has changed at the office. Things are going to get worse before they get better. They're going to make things miserable for me. But that doesn't matter. I've given it all to the Lord. That means I don't have to figure out all the details of my future." Then he added, "I'm going to relax now."

He was a good man in a hard place. But you wouldn't know what he was going through by looking at him. Somehow he grasped the great truth that praying "Thy will be done" means letting go of your own life. My friend learned it the same way we all have to learn it—through pain and difficulty and the hard times of life. As we were walking back to his car, he said, "Every day I pray this simple prayer, 'Thy will be done.'" No wonder he had a smile on his face. Praying that way means giving up control of your life. But that doesn't mean your life will go out of control. It just means that your life is surrendered to God's control.

This leads to some very practical questions:

1. Do I want to know God's will so I can consider it, or do I want to know God's will so I can do it?
2. Am I willing to be engulfed with God's will, or do I simply want help in making a hard decision?
3. Am I ready to love what He loves, to go where He sends me, to obey what He tells me to do, to suffer when that is required, to wait when that is required, to endure when that is required, and to rejoice when that is required?
4. Have I agreed with God in advance that I will do His will even before it is revealed to me?
5. Will I take the daily small steps that are before me while waiting for the big steps to be revealed?

6. Do I understand that the will of God is more about *who* I am on the inside than *where* I am on the outside?

7. Am I ready for my life to change if that's what needs to happen?

This is the heart of the prayer—that we might be filled to overflowing with the knowledge of God's will so that we want what God wants for us and we do what He wants us to do.

THE PURPOSE

Paul has only one purpose in mind. This purpose is the result of being filled with the knowledge of His will. And this purpose is not possible without coming to the place where we say, "Your will be done—nothing more, nothing less, nothing." We find it expressed this way in verse 10: **"And we pray this in order that you may live a life worthy of the Lord and may please him in every way."** This is an astonishing statement if you think about what it means. Note the word "worthy." It comes from a root that means "heaviness" or "weightiness." Sometimes, in evaluating certain people who don't measure up to our expectations, we call them "lightweights." A "lightweight" person is someone whose contribution is trifling and doesn't amount to much. All of us, if we are honest, think about our own value and worth from time to time. Since we aren't going to live forever, we want to know that our time in this world has mattered, that we didn't squander our opportunities, that we made a difference to someone, somewhere, somehow. And each one of us has personal failings, cracks in the soul, and hidden fissures of sin and failure and doubt and compromise that others don't know about. We may put up a good front and even smile bravely on Sunday morning, but deep inside we know that we are far from what we want to be. Sometimes those feelings of self-doubt may overwhelm us to the point where we wonder why we should even bother getting out of bed in the morning. But here we are called to something very exciting: to walk worthy of the Lord and so hear Him say, "My child, I am pleased with you in every way."

This doesn't happen automatically; therefore we must think carefully about what we believe. In Christ we have been fully accepted by God and adopted into His family. We have been blessed with every spiritual blessing already (2 Peter 1:3). There is a true sense in which God is pleased with us already because we are united by faith in His Son, and He is fully pleased with Jesus. In a related way, a parent will listen to a child play the trumpet and miss ten out of eleven notes. Everyone else winces, but Dad will beam and say, "That's my boy!" We understand that sort of family pride. But there is another sort of pride that comes when a son or daughter, through hard work and years of dedication, accomplishes some great goal and brings honor to the family name. That's what Paul has in mind here. It means to live so that God is pleased with us.

"Tell them about Jesus."

Rick Husband was the commander of the space shuttle *Columbia* that disintegrated over Texas on February 1, 2003. Everyone who knew him knew he was a Christian. Before the shuttle took off on January 16, Rick stopped the crew and prayed for them. NASA workers said that they had never before seen a commander pray with his crew. At T minus two minutes before liftoff, a NASA controller commented that it was a perfect day for launch, and Rick replied, "The Lord has given us a beautiful day." Before the flight, he left recorded devotional videos for each of his two children to watch each of the seventeen days he would be gone. Those thirty-four videos were recorded so his children would not miss their daily devotions with their dad. In a video made for his home church in Houston, he explained the values of his life: "If I ended up at the end of my life having been an astronaut, but having sacrificed my family along the way or living my life in a way that didn't glorify God, then I would look back on it with great regret. Having become an astronaut would not really have mattered all that much.

And I finally came to realize that what really meant the most to me was to try and live my life the way God wanted me to and to try and be a good husband to Evelyn and a good father to my children."

After the shuttle disaster, his pastor in Houston visited with Evelyn Husband. She showed the pastor documents Rick left in case something tragic happened on the mission and he did not return home. The documents contained personal messages to his family members. At the bottom of the documents, Husband wrote a special note to his pastor that said, "Tell them about Jesus. He means everything to me."

Rick Husband has gone to heaven, but while he was on the earth, he lived a life worthy of the Lord. No doubt he heard the Lord say, "Well done, good and faithful servant. Enter into the joy of the Lord."

When I read his story, I asked myself, "What is the secret of a man like Rick Husband? Where does faith like this come from?" I think I know the answer. Years ago he yielded control of his life to Jesus Christ. Everything else that happened to him flowed from that one great decision. Somewhere along the way, he told the Lord, "I want to do Your will. If it means being an astronaut, that's what I'll do. If it means going up in space and not coming home to my family, I am willing to do what You call me to do." I don't know if he said it in those words, but that was the commitment of his heart. You don't make the kind of impact he made without that kind of commitment. Rick Husband is gone, but he left behind a shining legacy. If we want to have a strong witness in life and after our death, we must first truly say, "O Lord, Your will be done in my life. No strings, no conditions, no special deals. I give You my life to do with as You will."

When we want what God wants, when we surrender our will and our agenda, and when His purposes become our purposes, then our lives will be dramatically changed. We will find purpose and meaning in everything that happens to us. Life becomes a daily adventure with God. When that happens, our lives become joyful, visibly different, and eternally significant. And God is pleased with us.

THE RESULTS

The remainder of the prayer involves four results that follow from walking worthy of God and pleasing Him in everything. First, we will have a life that bears fruit. **"Bearing fruit in every good work" (v. 10b)** presents a delightful picture of God producing His good fruit in us day by day. Fruit is the natural product of a fruit tree. If an apple tree doesn't produce apples, something is wrong. Seen in its broadest perspective, the "fruit" of the Christian life is nothing less than the life of Christ produced in us.

"I am the vine; you are the branches. If a man remains

in me and I in him, he will bear much fruit; apart from me you can do nothing" (John 15:5). *We* do not produce the "fruit" of a godly life; it is produced in us by the power of the Holy Spirit. We are called to do the "good work" that God puts before us every day. We get up, go to work, go to school, do our job, meet people, buy and sell, complete projects, fill our appointments, and check off the items on our to-do list. What that looks like for you won't be exactly the same for any other person. But we all have "good work" to do every day. That's part of being filled with the knowledge of God's will. We all understand that it's possible to do our jobs with a smile or with a frown. Life can be a chore, or it can be a joy. When we are truly surrendered to the Lord and are filled with the knowledge of His will, we don't mope our way through life, gritting our teeth just to make it through one more lousy morning. We bear the good "fruit of love, joy, peace, patience, kindness, goodness, faithfulness, gentleness, and self-control" that Paul talks about in Galatians 5:22–23.

I spoke with a young man who is just starting out in the business world. He managed to land an entry-level job with a large company and now finds himself frustrated. His job is boring, and the people he works with are irritating. The young man has great talent and will probably do well in his career, but right now he needs a major "attitude adjustment." He didn't believe it when I told him that more people are fired for a bad attitude than for poor performance. But it's true. It's not just *what* we do in life that counts; it's also *how* we do it. People watch Christians carefully because we claim to have a personal relationship with God. Unbelievers may not understand theology, but they do expect that our faith will make a difference in the way we do our work. That's where this prayer is so powerful. Once our lives are filled with the knowledge of God's will, we will bear the fruit of a changed life (a positive attitude being just one evidence of fruit) in the "good work" that we do.

Second, we will have a life that grows in the knowledge of God. This follows logically from being filled with the knowledge of God's will. Proverbs 3:6 tell us to "acknowledge" God, and He will make our paths straight. In the Hebrew text, the word "acknowledge" is an imperative—a command. You could translate this by saying, "In all your ways *know Him.*" Do you want to know the secret to knowing the will of God? If there is a "secret," here it is. In everything you do, know God. But we want a formula. We want three steps. God says, "Know Me. Spend time with Me. Put Me first in every area of your life. Trust Me to work out all things for good." Wow! Do you understand that this is a revolutionary way of looking at life?

A few years ago I heard someone say that many of the little decisions we agonize about won't matter at all in ten thousand years. That blew my mind at first.

What a liberating way to look at life. The next time you face a tough decision that seems enormously important to you at that moment, ask yourself if it will really matter in ten thousand years. Ninety-nine percent of what you worried about this week won't matter three weeks from now, much less ten thousand years from now. In the year 2452, it won't matter whether you lived in Minnesota, Santa Fe, or South Carolina. But what will matter is that you have decided in all your ways to know God. *In light of this prayer, the will of God for your life is to know God in everything. To see Him present everywhere and in everything, and to live in total surrender to Him.* The most important thing is not the decisions you face; the most important thing is your relationship with God. And the closer you are to God, the easier it will be for God to guide you in the way He wants you to go.

Third, we will have a life that endures in hard times. We will have **"great endurance and patience"** because we are **"being strengthened with all power according to his glorious might"** (v. 11). And the strength that comes will be an "inside job" that will enable us to endure with patience those things that might otherwise destroy us. A young mother who lost a child to Sudden Infant Death Syndrome wrote to say how God gave her and her husband strength in the year after their son's death: "You realize clearly that we don't know how much time any of us has on earth and that exits are surprising." Then she spoke of how other believers had prayed for them. "We know so many have been praying for us, and I can honestly say we felt it." One couple that didn't know them very well prayed that God would give them "extreme comfort." Eventually she met them. "We felt the extreme comfort, too. I do not believe we could have come through this past year so well without the prayers of so many people." They have been in a support group that includes non-Christians and have seen the difference that Christ makes. "One couple in the group is so angry at God and has had a miserable year. We have been able to let God comfort us and have a totally different perspective than many in the group. It is a blessing to see how God can work in a hard situation."

One Sunday night, about 11:30 P.M., I received a call from a woman whose husband had been slowly dying of cancer. She told me that he was not expected to live much longer. When I got to the hospital, the family was gathered around his bed. He did indeed appear to be nearing the end of his earthly life. He had struggled with cancer for several years and had been in a nursing home for the last year or so. And for years before that, he lived with various physical ailments. At one point this woman took her husband's hand and exclaimed, "God has been so good to us!"

That might seem like a strange statement when your spouse is at the point of death, but to her it was a natural expression of her faith in Christ. Through the years of hardship, the two of them had experienced the goodness and faithfulness of the Lord in so many ways. It is a great advance in the spiritual life to be able to see the goodness of the Lord even in life's darkest hour.

Fourth, we will have a life that gives thanks continually. To be specific, we will rejoice and give thanks that we have been taken out of the kingdom of darkness and been transferred into the kingdom of light. We will rejoice that we have a great inheritance with all the saints of God, so that in this life we have all that we need, and, in the life to come, we will see Jesus face-to-face and will enjoy all the glories of heaven. And we will never forget that all that God has for us comes through our Lord Jesus Christ, who redeemed us with His own blood.

It is a good thing if we never get over the wonder of our salvation. I received a wonderful e-mail from a man in his forties. After his parents divorced when he was fifteen, he began to drink heavily, and soon his drinking was out of control. In his twenties, he says that he "got involved with a girl from whom Delilah could have taken lessons. Some old friends gave lots of support, Jack Daniels, Jim Beam, 'Bud Weiser'." He served in the military in various hot spots around the world— Saudi Arabia, Somalia, South Korea—getting drunk every chance he had. He left the military but continued to drink heavily. Many years later he met a woman, they got married, and he and his wife began church-hopping. Meanwhile he continued to drink, thinking he had it "under control." Somehow they came to the church I pastor. "That Sunday we came to Calvary Memorial, the Bible Bus was in full gear in the book of Genesis and you seemed to be speaking to us as if we were the only people in the room. . . . For the first time I picked up the Bible and read it cover-to-cover. Along the way, I listed my sins, then confessed them to the Lord Jesus Christ and accepted Jesus as my Lord and Savior. I remember the feeling that radiated from me at that moment—for the first time I truly understood the term 'born again in Christ.'" Then he added these words: "Not only was I saved, but also the Lord has given me the strength to resist alcohol, and he has blessed us with a baby girl. Now a day doesn't go by when I don't thank the Lord for all the blessings over my lifetime and ask forgiveness for the times I took them for granted." Here is man who understands what it means to be transferred from one kingdom to another. For years he lived in darkness; now he lives in the light of God's love. No wonder he is grateful. That's what Paul means when he talks about "**joyfully giving thanks (vv. 11–12).**"

If you stand back and think about it, this is an amazing way to live—filled with good works, an ever-growing knowledge of God, the ability to endure hard times with joy, and a thankful spirit for all that God has done.

Again, here is the prayer. *Paul prays that we might be filled up to overflowing with the knowledge of God's will.* That means yielding our agenda to His control so that His purposes become our purposes. When that happens, our lives are radically changed from the inside out. We set out to please the Lord in everything. Suddenly, we become difference-makers in the world (like Rick Husband). We're involved in God's agenda, which means we're doing more than just taking up space until we die. Life now has purpose and meaning. We have a reason to get out of bed in the morning. We're linked with God in His kingdom work on the earth.

And all of this is because of Jesus Christ. He gave us an inheritance, so we know we have a great future. He took us out of the darkness, so now we can see things clearly. He made us citizens of His kingdom, so now we have everything we need. He redeemed us by His blood, so we know our sins are forgiven. Sometimes at the end of a TV program, you see a statement like this: "This program made possible by General Motors or IBM or Exxon." Perhaps we should add a sentence to the end of verse 14: "This prayer made possible by Jesus Christ." All that we have comes directly from Him.

While traveling not long ago, I had a chance to read *Wild at Heart* by John Eldredge.[1] It's a fine book about the search to discover the true purpose for a man's life. Toward the end of the book, the author relates that, while rummaging through a bookstore, his life was changed by two sentences in a book that he happened to pick up. Those two sentences were so insightful that he didn't read another word. "I set the volume down without turning another page and walked out of that bookstore to find a life worth living." Fascinating expression: a life worth living. Sounds a lot like the prayer in Colossians 1. This is what the book said: "Don't ask yourself what the world needs. Ask yourself what makes you come alive, and go do that, because what the world needs is people who have come alive." I've been pondering that ever since I read it. It seems profoundly true to me. What is it that makes you come alive? It is right here that Paul's prayer hits us right between the eyes. For too long we have thought the will of God was boring, dull, negative, tame—something like homework for algebra class. You have to do it, but you don't have to like it. How wrong we are! To be filled with God's will means that we are finally free to come alive. To be filled with God's will means we are finally free to fulfill our destiny. To be filled with God's will means we are free from the tyranny of following the world's agenda for us. To be filled with God's will means we are free to risk everything for the sake of Christ and His Kingdom. *If you ever decide to seek God's will, your life may be many things, but it won't be boring.* The man was right. The world needs people who have come alive. I would simply add that the world needs people who have come alive to the knowledge of God's will. And that's a fitting description of the people who pray this prayer.

Lord Jesus, fill me with the knowledge of Your will so that I want what You want. Bring me to the place where I will say, "Your will be done—nothing less, nothing more, nothing else." Help me to live so that You are pleased, and others may know that I know You. I pray that I might know You better so that when hard times come, I will have the strength to be faithful and not turn away. Grant me a grateful heart as I recall what You have done for me. As your child, I belong with You, Lord, in Your eternal kingdom, with all the redeemed people of God. I thank You that You rescued me from the darkness of my sins. Hasten the day when I will be by Your side, worshiping you, fully engaged in praising Your name. Until then, make my heart come alive with the knowledge of Your will. Let me not shirk my duties, but love others, pray for them, encourage them, and show them the highest and best way to live. Amen.

EPHESIANS 1:15–23

✠

"For this reason, ever since I heard about your faith in the Lord Jesus and your love for all the saints, I have not stopped giving thanks for you, remembering you in my prayers. I keep asking that the God of our Lord Jesus Christ, the glorious Father, may give you the Spirit of wisdom and revelation, so that you may know him better. I pray also that the eyes of your heart may be enlightened in order that you may know the hope to which he has called you, the riches of his glorious inheritance in the saints, and his incomparably great power for us who believe. That power is like the working of his mighty strength, which he exerted in Christ when he raised him from the dead and seated him at his right hand in the heavenly realms, far above all rule and authority, power and dominion, and every title that can be given, not only in the present age but also in the one to come. And God placed all things under his feet and appointed him to be head over everything for the church, which is his body, the fullness of him who fills everything in every way."

3

OPEN MY EYES, LORD

I wonder if we would be happy if our prayers were published so that others could read them. That's a fascinating thought, isn't it? What if all of the prayers that you ever prayed, word for word, were accessible so that anyone, anywhere could read them? Would our prayers be worth reading if they were posted on the Internet? And would they be like those found in the pages of Holy Scripture, or would they more likely fit the *National Enquirer?*

In this book we're looking at the "published" prayers of the apostle Paul. It takes a certain amount of courage to write down your prayers, but these prayers deserve to be studied because they are unlike most of our prayers. As we study these prayers, we are going to discover new patterns of prayer that will help us align our hearts with God's will and trust Him the way that He deserves to be trusted. If we want the Lord to teach us to pray, this is a good place to start. *Paul's prayers set a very high standard, which, if followed, would radically transform our own prayers. After all, prayer is the thermometer of the soul.* If you want to know what someone believes, don't tell me what he says; tell me what he prays. A person may say many things, but when he prays, his heart is fully revealed.

With that in mind, we turn to the prayer of Paul in Ephesians 1:15–23. Before we jump into the text, I have a confession to make. For many years (twenty-five years at least) whenever I read this prayer, it was always very difficult for me to understand. For one thing, in the Greek text, verses 15–23 constitute one long, complex sentence, filled with phrases and clauses piled on top of each other. It's easy to get lost in the details and miss the message. But it would be a shame to discount it simply because it seems complex. If we did, we'd miss out on a really amazing prayer. If it starts as a whisper, it ends in a roar. What starts as a trickling mountain stream becomes a mighty torrent of truth by the end. It wasn't until recently that I saw how simple this prayer really is.

The key is at the end of verse 17 where Paul says, **"That you may know him better."** That's it! That's the essence of the whole prayer right there. Paul is praying that the Ephesians might know God better. This means that he is writing to and praying for believers who already have some knowledge of God. His central request is, "O Lord, I pray that these folks who already know You might come to a new and deeper knowledge of who You really are." The Greek language contains a number of different words that might be translated as "know." This particular verse contains a verb that means to know deeply, personally, intimately. For instance, I know President Bush. I know who he is and what he looks like. If you show me his picture, I'll say, "That's President Bush." But I don't know him personally, and he doesn't know me from Adam's housecat. But I can also say, "I know my wife." That's an entirely different kind of knowing. After thirty years of marriage, it is a knowledge that is very deep, very personal, and very intimate. Paul prayed that the Ephesians might have exactly that sort of intimate knowledge of God.

Ephesians 1:3–14 constitutes one long doxology of praise to God. That doxology is followed by this long prayer that they might know God better. Think of it this way: *Paul puts the truth out, and then he prays the truth in.* In verse 3 he says we have been blessed with every spiritual blessing. So the prayer is not, "Lord, give us new blessings," but, "Help us to realize the blessings we already have." Not, "Give us new truth," but, "Help us experience the truth we already know." Spiritual truth can be academic and cold and formal. So he's praying, "Lord, turn them on to the truth. Lord, they know You, now make them excited about knowing you."

THE REQUEST

"**I keep asking that the God of our Lord Jesus Christ, the glorious Father, may give you the Spirit of wisdom and revelation, so that you may know him better**" (Ephesians 1:17). Three things strike me as I ponder verse 17. The first is the phrase "I keep asking." Paul did not believe that if you made a prayer request, you never had to make it again. When Paul prayed for the Ephesians, he prayed the same request over and over again—that they would know God better. Sometimes I hear it said that since God knows everything we say before we say it and everything we think before we think it (which is true), that we should never repeat ourselves in prayer (which is not true). *We don't pray to inform God of anything.* He knows what we are thinking long before we voice our prayers to him. But if he knows all, why pray at all? The simple answer is one you have heard before: "He's God, and we're not." We pray to express our total dependence on Him for everything. As we continue to pray for the same things for our loved ones over and over again, the godly desires of the heart grow stronger, and we are reminded that every day we must be one hundred percent dependent on God. We can't live on yesterday's blessings, and we can't depend on yesterday's prayers. So just like Paul, we "keep asking" on behalf of our loved ones.

The second thing I notice is that only God can give us what we truly need. If we are Christians, the Holy Spirit lives within us, but we must pray that the Holy Spirit will grant us the wisdom we need to understand the things of God. Education alone will never meet our deepest needs. Most of us have knowledge coming out of our ears. We have sermons and tapes and CDs and Christian radio and Christian TV and books and videos and conferences and notebooks crammed with information. If knowledge alone would make us holy, we would be honorary apostles. But we need the Holy Spirit to do what only the Spirit can do—give us wisdom and revelation to make the truth come alive in our hearts.

The third thing I notice is the request itself—to know God better. That's simple and clear, isn't it? I received an e-mail from a friend whose family has endured a very difficult trial in the last several years. He wrote to say how the ordeal has changed his view of what it means to know God. There are three levels of knowing God, he wrote. First, there is the level of experience. All of us who know the Lord have some experiences with Him that we can use to help others. Second, there is the level of knowledge. This can come from going to church, listening to sermons, reading the Bible and good books, or studying in a Christian school. But there is a third level, which he called the level of wisdom. This level comes only by prayer. He offers this very helpful insight about a level three relationship with God: "We begin to see things through God's eyes and less through our eyes. Peace only comes from this level. It is not measurable, explainable, nor understandable. Levels one and two are not prerequisites. I see prayer lifting the illiterate to great places of peace and wisdom, where certain people with Ph.D.s in religion may feel empty. Our prayers become less 'gimme' and more 'help me see what You want me to learn through this' to 'deepen my relationship with You.'" Then he included the words of the old hymn *Sweet Hour of Prayer*.[1] Although I had heard it and sung it many times, one verse stuck in my mind as especially appropriate:

> *Sweet hour of prayer, sweet hour of prayer,*
> *Thy wings shall my petition bear,*
> *To him whose truth and faithfulness*
> *Engage the waiting soul to bless;*
> *And since he bids me seek his face,*

Believe his word and trust his grace,
I'll cast on him my every care,
And wait for thee, sweet hour of prayer.

As I ponder what my friend wrote in light of what Paul said, the thought came to me that this sort of knowledge of God is available to everyone, but it is not automatic. It would be possible, I suppose, to come up with "Three Steps to a Deeper Knowledge of God," and such a list could be helpful in one sense. But Paul never makes a list like that. We must sincerely seek to know God better. It doesn't happen by accident. That's why this prayer is so vital. And my friend is right that too many of us live with merely a level two knowledge of God. We think that reading books (like this one) will increase our knowledge of God. Speaking as an author, I hope this book helps you in many ways, but I know for certain that reading my words will not automatically bring you closer to God. That's a matter of the heart that my words cannot touch. Many of us ought to pray like this: "Lord, I have heard so much truth. Now open my eyes, and let me see You."

Here's a piece of good news: *God invites us to seek His face. He wants us to know Him better.* It's not as if our heavenly Father is hiding Himself from us. But we can have a close relationship with Him only if we seek it in prayer. That's the burden of Paul's prayer—for a level three relationship with God that doesn't depend on knowledge or experience but comes through wisdom and seeking the Lord. Any of us can have that sort of relationship with God if we want it and if we are willing to pay the price to have it.

THE MEANS

"I pray also that the eyes of your heart may be enlightened" (Ephesians 1:18a). This is the heart of the prayer. It is also the only time the phrase "the eyes of your heart" appears in the New Testament. The heart has eyes. Did you know that? When Paul speaks of "your heart," he's not referring to the organ in your chest that pumps blood throughout your body. The term "heart" refers to what we might call "the real you," the place inside where the decisions of life are made. The heart is the place where you decide what values you will live by and what direction you will go and how you will live your life each day. Every important decision you make is made by your heart. And your heart has eyes that can be opened or shut. When the eyes of your heart are closed to the light of God, you stumble blindly through life, making one dumb choice after another. You fall into sinful patterns, break God's laws, end up driving into the ditch, and enter one dead-end relationship after another. Why? When the eyes of your heart are shut, you lack moral vision. You can have

20/20 vision with your physical eyes, but the eyes of your heart can be blind to the light of God. There are lots of people like that in the world. We see this principle when we witness to those who don't know Christ. After sharing the gospel with them, sometimes they will say, "I just don't see it." That's not an excuse; they truly don't see it. *You can talk to a lost person until you are blue in the face, and it will do no good if the eyes of his heart aren't open.* You can quote Billy Graham, Josh McDowell, Francis Schaeffer, and, if you're creative, you can throw in some John Calvin and Martin Luther. Quote Abraham Lincoln and Mike Ditka if you like. It will do no good. You can quote Scripture all day long, and the lost will still be lost. Until their eyes are opened, they will not "see" the truth about Christ.

What is the answer? We must pray for the lost that God will open their eyes, give life in place of death, enable them to hear, create within them a desire to understand, give them a hunger for Jesus, and then grant them faith to believe the gospel. In short, as we prepare to share Christ with others, we must fervently pray that God will go before us. When we pray for the lost, we are saying to God, "You go first! If You don't go first, all our efforts will be in vain."

And sometimes there are Christians who need to have their eyes opened by the Lord. They know God, but their eyes are so filled with the things of the world that they are blind to the truth. Let's say that we have a Christian young man who has been raised in a Christian home. He's been going to church for years—Sunday school, vacation Bible school, children's ministry, AWANA, and youth group. Now he goes off to college, and at last he's on his own. He meets a girl, and they start dating. Soon they are sleeping together. When his parents hear about it, they are furious and worried and upset, and they wonder what to do. They argue and plead and cajole and threaten and quote Scripture—all to no avail. What is the problem? It is precisely this: The eyes of the heart are shut to the truth of God. And until those eyes are opened, all the yelling in the world won't make much difference.

But at this point we encounter a liberating truth in our text. Paul prayed for the Ephesians that "the eyes of your heart might be opened." One translation says, "that the eyes of your heart might be flooded with light." *Opening blind eyes is the supernatural work of the Holy Spirit.* He and He alone can do it. But He can do it, and this is the source of our hope. This is why we pray for our children and grandchildren and family members and friends and loved ones who today are far from God. As our children grow older, we discover over and over again how little control we have over them. We cannot compel their obedience because we cannot compel their hearts. But we can pray and cry out to God and say, "O Lord, open the eyes of their heart. Help them to see the light of truth."

It's a good thing to come to the place where you can release your children to the Lord. I was sitting by myself in the airport, and my flight was delayed. A woman named Sharon took the seat next to me. She introduced herself and started chatting with me. When she found out I was flying to New York to teach Galatians, she said that she had been in a Bible study with some women from her neighborhood.

She and her husband are farmers in a midwestern state. She was traveling east to visit her son. At this point the story gets a bit complicated. She and her husband have two sons, both of them raised in the Christian faith, but neither son attends church at this point. The son she was going to visit lives in a house with a woman he used to date years ago. The woman was never married but has a child by someone else. Sharon's son and the woman he once dated are still good friends. The woman's child is six years old, and Sharon loves her as if she were her own granddaughter. Plus there is another man who lives in the same house. I guess he's a friend of Sharon's son and of the woman. The son and the woman he once dated are not "living together" in the usual sense of that phrase. So I said, trying to piece it all together, it's sort of like the TV show *Three's Company*, only with two guys and a girl. Yes, sort of, Sharon said with a smile. Her son and the woman don't plan to get married, but the son says neither one of them is likely to marry anyone else given their current housing arrangements. And, to be precise, Sharon was flying to Baltimore to take care of the "granddaughter" because the mother works for the government and was flying to Iceland for some sort of high-level conference. I think that about covers it. I told Sharon that I barely understood it all and didn't think I could diagram it on paper.

When all is said and done, Sharon's greatest desire is to see her son rededicate his life to the Lord. She had wrestled with all of the other details and complicating circumstances until one day the Lord told her, "Sharon, you just love him. I'll change him." And that's what she decided to do. Since then, everything has gone much better. "I just love him, and I let the Lord take care of everything else," she said with a smile.

And a big part of loving our children, especially our wayward children, is to pray, "Lord, open the eyes of their heart so that the light of Your truth can come flooding in."

CHRIST AT THE CENTER OF LIFE

When Eugene Peterson translated the last part of this prayer in Ephesians for THE MESSAGE, he included this unique sentence: "At the center of all this, Christ rules the church. The church, you see, is not peripheral to the world; the world is peripheral to the church." There are two radically different ways of looking at things. Either (1) the world is at the center, and Christ is at the periphery, or (2) Christ is at the center of life, and the world is off at the edges. So many Christians have bought into the notion that this world is all that matters. They've pushed Christ to the periphery of life. But when Christ comes to the center, the world is seen for what it really is—something on the edges.

Not long ago I talked with a friend who was struggling with this very issue. I explained that living for Christ is like a football game. You're either on the bench or in the game. "Your problem is, you're sitting on the bench goofing off when you ought to be in the game serving the Lord. Benchwarmers sit around, goof off, laugh, and trade jokes while the game is going on. If you ever decide to get in the game, you won't have time to do the things you do now."

If our young people sleep around, if they get drunk on the weekends, if they cheat and cut corners, or if they are rebellious and unmotivated, those things are only symptoms of a deeper, more fundamental issue. They've never made a personal commitment to get serious about Jesus Christ. They're sitting on the bench when they ought to be in the game. And I say this with total certainty, once you get into the game, once Christ becomes the center of life, no one will have to tell you not to sleep around. No one will have to tell you, "Don't get drunk on the weekends." You just won't do it. Christian, once the eyes of your heart are opened, the light of God's truth will come flooding in, and you'll never look at anything the same away again.

Sometimes we worry too much about the symptoms without dealing with the root issues of life. We ought to pray for God to open the eyes of the heart. When that happens, life will radically change. The heart changes first, then the outward actions follow. *Then* a person will grab his helmet and get in the ball game for the Lord. Then he will get into the huddle and say, "You call the play, Lord. I'm ready to do whatever You say."

THE RESULTS

As Paul prays, he has three things specifically in mind that will result from the eyes of the heart being opened.

They Will Know All That God Has Given

"The hope to which he has called you" (Ephesians 1:18b). This looks back to the moment of their conversion. Verses 3–14 list some elements of that hope:

Blessed with every spiritual blessing, v. 3

Chosen in Christ, v. 4

Predestined to be adopted as sons, v. 5

Recipients of His grace, v. 6

Redeemed through His blood, v. 7

Forgiveness of sins, v. 7

Wisdom and understanding, v. 8

God's plan made known to us, vv. 9–10

Chosen and predestined, v. 11

Included in Christ, v. 13

Sealed by the Holy Spirit, v. 13

Given the earnest of the Spirit, v. 14

All this is ours. It is the permanent possession of every child of God. We are rich and blessed beyond all measure. Paul prays that we might understand how rich we already are.

They Will Know All That God Has Promised

"The riches of his glorious inheritance in the saints" (Ephesians 1:18c). This looks ahead to the end of time when we will see the Lord face-to-face and receive all that He has promised us. *It is beyond our capacity to describe the glory of meeting the Lord.* Sometimes we wonder what heaven will be like. I think it will be everything we dreamed of and nothing like we imagined. Going to heaven is not so much going to a place as it is going to a person. If I've been away speaking for a week, I may say to someone, "I can't wait to get home again." But I'm not talking about the literal bricks and carpet. It's not as if when I come in, I say, "Hello, drapes, I'm glad to see you again. Hello, dining room, I missed sitting in those chairs." You'd think something was wrong if I talked like that. No, home is precious to me because of the people I love who live there. When I say, "I can't wait to go home," I mean that I can't wait to see Marlene and Josh and Mark and Nick again. It's the same thing with heaven. The glory of heaven is not the streets of gold or the gates of pearl or even the river of life or the angels of God. The glory of heaven is Jesus. Heaven is where Jesus is, and when we finally get there, we will be home for all eternity.

They Will Know All That God Has Provided

"His incomparably great power for us who believe" (Ephesians 1:19a). There are four different Greek words for power here. Paul uses the word from which we get "dynamite" and the word from which we get "energy." He uses a word that means "muscular strength" and another that means "courageous power." *God's power is sufficient for all we need.* Often we are gripped by fear, inadequacy, insecurity, and a feeling that we are powerless to change things. The good news is that God's power is wrapped up in a person, Jesus Christ. This is the power that exploded in Christ when

He rose from the dead. If you know Him, you have the greatest power source in the universe living within you.

Not long ago I was asked to visit a woman in my church who was dying of cancer. She looked so frail, but her husband said that she perked right up when she heard my voice outside her door. It was obvious to me that the end was near. Speaking was difficult so I held her hand and recited the great promises of God about heaven. Someone in the room said that this lady was afraid to die. I told her that I wasn't an expert on death, but I know someone who is. I told her I know someone who had died and come back from the dead. His name is Jesus. He holds the keys of death and Hades in His hand. When the moment comes, don't be afraid. Call out the name Jesus, and He will come for you. I told her that I don't know about death by personal experience, but I know who stands at the door to make sure we make it safely through to the other side. Then I quoted the familiar words of the Twenty-third Psalm, "Yea, though I walk through the valley of the shadow of death, I will fear no evil: for thou art with me; thy rod and thy staff, they comfort me . . . Surely goodness and mercy shall follow me all the days of my life: and I shall dwell in the house of the Lord forever" (Psalm 23:4, 6 KJV). After I prayed, someone in the room started to sing, "What a friend we have in Jesus . . ." We all started singing, and I heard my friend in the hospital bed singing with us in a frail voice. But there was a smile on her face. At death's door, she was holding on to Jesus. A few days later she met Him face-to-face.

PRAY, AND KEEP ON PRAYING

Why should we worry? Why should we fear? Why should we doubt? *Our God has given us all we need.* Oh, that we might know the hope of our calling, the riches of our inheritance, and the amazing power of God. It's all ours and wrapped up in one person, Jesus Christ. Let's pray that we might know Him better, that our eyes might be opened to see things clearly, and that we might love Him and serve Him and make Him the center of our lives.

What a magnificent encouragement this passage is. Pray, pray, and keep on praying. Pray for each other. Husbands, pray for your wives. Wives, pray for your husbands. Pray for the class you teach. Pray for the new Christians you are discipling. Pray that they will be turned on by the truth of God.

The prayer we've been looking at can guide you in praying for your children too. How long should we pray for them? And what should we pray for them? The first answer is, never stop praying for your children. Paul said, "I keep on asking." We can always know God better than we do. And, second, when you pray for these young people, ask the Lord to open the eyes of their hearts to let His light come flooding in.

"O Lord, help me to know You better. Open my eyes, Lord. Let Your light come flooding into my heart. Help me to know all that You have given, all that You have promised, and all that You have provided for me. Forgive me for hearing the truth so often and not being changed by it. May Christ be at the center of my life, now and forever. Amen."

EPHESIANS 3:14—21

✠

"For this reason I kneel before the Father, from whom his whole family in heaven and on earth derives its name. I pray that out of his glorious riches he may strengthen you with power through his Spirit in your inner being, so that Christ may dwell in your hearts through faith. And I pray that you, being rooted and established in love, may have power, together with all the saints, to grasp how wide and long and high and deep is the love of Christ, and to know this love that surpasses knowledge—that you may be filled to the measure of all the fullness of God. Now to him who is able to do immeasurably more than all we ask or imagine, according to his power that is at work within us, to him be glory in the church and in Christ Jesus throughout all generations, for ever and ever! Amen."

4

BEYOND
YOUR DREAMS

Martin Luther, the father of the Protestant Reformation, had a good friend and assistant by the name of Friedrich Myconius. In 1540, Myconius became sick and was expected to die. On his deathbed he wrote a tender farewell message to Luther. When Luther read the message, he immediately sent a reply: "I command thee in the name of God to live because I still have need of thee in the work of reforming the church. . . . The Lord will never let me hear that thou art dead, but will permit thee to survive me. For this I am praying, this is my will, and may my will be

BEYOND ALL YOU COULD ASK OR THINK

done, because I seek only to glorify the name of God."[1]
While those words might seem bold and brash, the
fact is that Myconius, who had already lost the ability
to speak when Luther's reply came, soon recovered
from his illness and lived six more years. He died two
months after Luther did. What an amazing testimony
to the power of prayer. Wouldn't you like to be able to
pray like that? I would!

One of the best ways to learn how to pray is to
study the prayers of the Bible. By listening in across the
centuries, we learn a great deal about the content of
biblical prayer and the intensity with which we should
pray. *The idea of praying with intensity may be new to
some people.* Many contemporary Christians find
themselves easily distracted when they attempt to pray.
If the truth were told, often we are playing around at
our prayers instead of approaching prayer with a holy
intensity. How different this is from the prayers of
Moses or Daniel or David or Paul. These men of God
prayed with fire in their souls. They cried out to God
with a single-minded focus that seemed to shut out the
world around them.

THE WINDOW OF THE SOUL

There is a great lesson here if we care to take it to
heart. *Prayer is truly the window of the soul.* What we
pray for, we care for. And the reverse is also true. What

we don't pray about, we don't care about. That's a solemn and convicting thought, and though we may try to escape its magnitude, we cannot escape the truth. We can say all we want about how much something means to us, but if we never bring it before God in prayer, we cannot truly say that we care deeply about it. We pray about what concerns us.

At least three things hold us back in the area of prayer. First, we fear that we don't pray often enough. Second, we worry that we won't use the right words, or we fear we'll say the wrong thing. Third, we think we don't have enough faith. Or, more accurately, we're sure we don't have enough faith to be heard by God. That's why the Bible records the prayers of great saints of God. We listen as Moses beseeches the Lord, as Nehemiah and Daniel intercede with the Almighty. In John 17 we observe the Lord Jesus talking intimately with His heavenly Father. And scattered throughout the Epistles, we find numerous short prayers by the apostle Paul. These biblical prayers are models and examples. They are not forms to be slavishly followed but guides to help us frame our thoughts as we come before the Lord in prayer. If we need help in prayer (and we do!), then we will be richly blessed as we study the prayers of the Bible.

I am especially grateful that Paul wrote the prayer we find in Ephesians 3:14–21. Beyond question, this is one of the greatest prayers in the entire Bible. One writer called it "the Holy of Holies in the Christian life." Another writer called it "a prayer for the impossible." This is the second prayer in Ephesians. We looked at the prayer in Ephesians 1 in the last chapter. There Paul prayed that the eyes of the heart might be opened to know God better. If the first prayer is for *enlightenment,* the second prayer is for *enablement.* If the first prayer is for knowledge, the second is for power.

THE REQUEST

It's easy to get lost in the details of this prayer. At first reading, it appears to be a complex arrangement of phrases piled one on top of the other, leading to a powerful doxology in verses 20–21. If we look at it that way, we'll miss the main point. A better way to study this prayer is to focus on the main request in verse 16 where Paul prays that God might "**strengthen you with power through his Spirit in your inner being.**" This is a prayer for spiritual strength in the inner being (literally, in Greek, the "inner man"). Paul prays for one main thing in this prayer. He asks God to strengthen the Ephesians by the Holy Spirit on the inside so that they can fulfill God's will. Though this prayer has many parts and builds to a big climax, there is only one basic request. Keep that in mind as we look at this text together.

How can I be so sure that there is only one basic request? The key is found in verse 13, just before the prayer begins: "I ask you, therefore, not to be discouraged because of my sufferings for you, which are your glory." The phrase "not to be discouraged" can be translated "not to lose heart" or "not to give up." This is extremely relevant because so many things sap our strength: discouraging circumstances, monotonous routine, physical weakness, personal failure, unwanted interruptions, unfinished responsibilities, and unresolved conflicts. Any one of those things can knock us out of commission, but often two or three of them hit us at the same time. And then we are knocked to the floor and find it hard to get up and get back in the fight. Tom Landry, longtime coach of the Dallas Cowboys, was fond of remarking, "Fatigue makes cowards of us all." Most of us can handle a little bit of adversity, and some of us can handle a lot of adversity, but everyone has a breaking point.

I discovered that truth in a very personal way a few months ago when I said to my congregation, "You're not as strong as you think you are, and neither am I." Little did I know how true those words would prove to be. A few days later I spent a week preaching in Florida. I wasn't feeling that great before I started, and I more or less collapsed after my last sermon. Since I have been sick only once in the last thirty years, I was unprepared for what happened to me. There was a fever and what seemed like the flu that morphed into a serious infection that caused me to miss my first Sunday in seventeen years because of sickness. In the midst of the illness, my mother died at the age of eighty-one. Although her health had been declining, the timing of her death was a surprise. And, like so many people before me, I can testify that even if you expect it, you're never really ready for the death of a parent. So we rounded up the boys and made a quick trip to Alabama where I had the privilege of speaking at my mother's graveside service. We buried her next to my father who died twenty-nine years earlier. The whole experience was like a blur in my mind, a "wrinkle in time" where the past, present, and the future seemed to come together for one fleeting moment. Then it was home and a recovery period that lasted for months. The following picture came to mind as I thought about the breaking points of life. The mightiest oak tree in the forest looks invincible, but if you hit it in just the right place with a tiny ax, it comes crashing down. The ax may be small, but it can bring down a tree in just a few seconds.

Seen in that light, this is a prayer for something most of us desperately need every day—spiritual strength. When we feel weak, prayer can be difficult or almost impossible. In those moments, here is a prayer that is always appropriate. It is a prayer to pray before you faint. If you are on the verge of giving up, take this prayer to heart before you throw in the towel. When you are weak, you need strength. And strength is the exact opposite of "losing heart" in verse 13. To be "strengthened with power" means to be made powerfully strong so that you can overcome the obstacles before you. The word for power is *dunamis,* from which we get the English words "dynamic" and "dynamite". When you are made strong in the inner man by the Holy Spirit, there will be power to blast out unbelief, to overcome despair, to rise above anger, and to keep going when you would rather quit. Note that this power is put to work in the "inner self," or the "inner man." That "inner man" is the control room of life where every great decision is made. This is the place where we need the most help.

"Lord, This Hurts"

As I pondered this prayer, it occurred to me how different it is from most that I hear (and to be honest, from most prayers I pray).

Most of our prayers fall into two categories:

1. Pain-avoidance. "Lord, this hurts. Make it stop."
2. Change of circumstances. "Lord, I don't like this. Change it, please."

Every time I have mentioned this in church, I am struck by the knowing smiles that spread across the congregation. No one likes pain, and no one enjoys difficult circumstances. It's natural to pray that your pain would stop and that your circumstances would improve—and it is not wrong to pray that way. The problem is, those two categories can overwhelm all our prayers so that we never pray for anything else. Yet Paul never mentions anything remotely related to either category. By the way, do you know where Paul was when he wrote Ephesians? He was in prison in Rome. Most authorities think he was chained at all times to two Roman guards. Yet he never mentions his imprisonment until almost the end of the epistle (Ephesians 6:20). And his request is not, "Pray that I will get out of here," but rather, "Pray that I will be bold for Christ even though I am in chains."

"You're Only Human"

Why does he pray for strengthening by the Spirit in the inner man? Because our greatest need is for spiritual power on the inside. No believer ever advances so far that he doesn't need God's power. As I thought about this fact, I remembered my dear friends from Texas, Jerry and Betty Formanek. Betty was a sweet spirit who always wanted to encourage me in my ministry. Almost every Sunday she said the same thing to me. If I heard her say it once, I guess I heard it a hundred times. Sometimes she would pat my arm as she said it. "Pastor Ray, remember, you're only human." At first I thought it was funny. Then it sort of drove me nuts. But much later I realized how profound it was. She was right. I am only human. And so are you. That means we're all in the same boat. All of us desperately need the Holy Spirit to strengthen us on the inside.

> I'm not as hot as I think I am.
> I'm not as strong as I think I am.
> I'm not as wise as I think I am.
> I'm not as resilient as I think I am.
> I'm not as resourceful as I think I am.
> I'm not as good as I think I am.

So the prayer is not, "Lord, take away my burdens," but rather, "Lord, give me stronger shoulders to carry the load." *It is a prayer for spiritual strength to do the work God gives us to do.* We especially need this in three areas:

1. To do our daily tasks with joy.
2. To resist temptation with courage.
3. To endure persecution gladly.

"This is my path, Lord, the path You have chosen for me. Make me powerfully strong in the inner man to walk where You are leading." That's the heart of this magnificent prayer. Everything else flows from this basic request.

THE RESULTS

The rest of the passage reveals the three results that come to us as we are strengthened by the Spirit on the inside.

Christ Dwelling in Our Hearts by Faith

The first great result is found in verse 17a: "**That Christ may dwell in your hearts through faith.**" The word "dwell" comes from a Greek word that itself is made up of two smaller words, one meaning "down" and the other meaning "home." The prayer is that Christ might be "down home" in your heart. It's the picture of a man at home in his own house. We all know there is a difference between a house and a home. A house is a building; a home is a dwelling place. It is very possible for Christ to be "in" your heart but not "at home" there. Let me illustrate. Suppose I go to visit a very nice home. The lady of the house says, "Pastor Ray, make yourself at home." I look around and appreciate the beauty of the home as I survey how nicely everything is arranged. It is lovely in all respects, but I do not feel at home there. I don't know where anything is. I don't know where the bathroom is. I don't know where the living room is. I don't know where the computers are. And (most important) I don't know where the remote control is. How can a man be at home if he can't find the remote control? If you come to my house, you'll see a man fully at home. I know where everything is, and if I don't know where it is, I know where to look for it. And you can rest assured that when the Super Bowl comes on, I'll know exactly where the remote control is because it will be right beside me.

Imagine your heart as a home with many rooms. There is a living room, dining room, bedroom, kitchen, computer room, TV room, attic, and closets. All of us have special rooms that we reserve for entertaining our guests. Most of us also have closets, basements, and attics that we try to keep out of public view because they are messy or contain items we don't want others to see. The same is true in the spiritual realm. Many of us have welcomed Christ into a large part of our hearts. But there are areas of life that He is not welcome to enter. It might be the kitchen or the bedroom or the recreation room that we keep locked from public view. Too many believers keep Christ in the entryway, as if to say, "Jesus, I've got You in the door. Now stay there and don't bother the rest of my life." But the Lord wants to enter every room. He wants to enter your kitchen, your bedroom, your library, your TV room, your computer room, and He wants access to every closet and even the attic of your heart. As long as you keep the doors locked, He can never be "at home" in your heart. And you will never be happy as a Christian. Usually there is some hidden sin—anger or bitterness or greed or lust or theft or jealousy or promiscuous behavior—that we would be ashamed for the Lord Jesus to see. Perhaps we don't want Him rearranging that part of our lives. Perhaps we like things the way they are. But we will never be happy, and Christ will never be fully at home until every door is opened to Him.

The question is not, "How much of the Lord do I have?" but rather, "How much of me does the Lord have?" O Christ, come in and purify my mind, ennoble my thoughts, guide my lips, and direct my path. This, then, is a prayer for a deeper experience between Christ and the believer. Call it what you will—sanctification, the "second blessing," total surrender, dedication, or even a filling of the Spirit. I call it "what we desperately need that most of us lack." Until Christ is at home in your heart, He will always seem like a stranger to you even though He lives in you. This is the first result of being strengthened in the inner man by the Holy Spirit.

> He's not just watching me, He's with me.
> He's not just with me, He's in me.
> He's not just a visitor, He's at home in my heart.

Growing Comprehension of the Love of Christ

"And I pray that you, being rooted and established in love, may have power, together with all the saints, to grasp how wide and long and high and deep is the

love of Christ, and to know this love that surpasses knowledge" (Ephesians 3:17b–19a). The second great result of being strengthened by the Spirit in the inner man is that you will have a growing comprehension of the love of Christ. The Greek word translated "grasp" has the idea of holding on to something. It means a growing personal experience of love of Jesus Christ. There is a sense in which all Christians experience the love of Christ. But love itself has many dimensions. In essence, Paul is saying, *"I pray that you may grow in your daily experience of the love of Jesus that you will come to know (in a personal way) this love that surpasses knowledge."* No matter how far you go in your knowledge of Christ's love, you will never come to the end of it.

Let me illustrate. When a man and woman meet and date and fall in love, their love is real and true, but it is not complete. On their wedding night, they will experience love in a deeper way, but there is much more to come. As the years go by, romantic love gives way to a love that springs from a deep, personal commitment made stronger and more profound by the changing seasons of life. And so a husband may truly say on his tenth anniversary, "Sweetheart, I love you more today than the day we got married." That is more than poetry or sentiment. In a good marriage, that is reality. My wife and I have been married thirty years. That's a long time to be married. It's long enough that we've been married longer than we were single. I can say without hesitation that it is better today than ever. Our marriage is stronger and happier and more satisfying than ten or fifteen or twenty years ago. How that happened I could not say, but it is true, and I am happy to say it. And I pray the Lord gives us at least another thirty years together.

Now take that principle into the spiritual realm, and you will understand what Paul means by the breadth and length and height and depth of the love of Christ. The early church took this as a sign of the cross. The "breadth and length" stood for the crossbar on which the arms of Christ were nailed. The "height and depth" stood for the vertical piece to which His legs were nailed. It is a fitting image because nowhere is the love of Christ more clearly seen than at the cross where Jesus died for us. Dr. W. A. Criswell liked to talk about "God's love in four dimensions" from John 3:16:

> "For God so loved the world"—
>   Breadth: "He included you."
> "That he gave his Son"—
>   Length: "He sent Jesus to die for you."
> "Should not perish"—
>   Depth: "He reached down for you."
> "Have everlasting life"—
>   Height: "He lifts you up to heaven."[2]

Christ's love is broader than the universe, longer than time, higher than hope, deeper than death. As we are strengthened by the Spirit on the inside, we will come to a new comprehension of Christ's love for us.

Fullness of God in Your Life

"That you may be filled to the measure of all the fullness of God" (Ephesians 3:19b). This is the whole goal of the Christian life. Don't water it down. The word for "filled" has the idea of being dominated by something. If you are filled with rage, then rage will dominate your life. If you are filled with love, then love dominates your life. If you are filled with joy, then joy dominates your life. When you are filled with God, then God Himself will dominate your life. *The human personality can be totally transformed by virtue of the presence of God.* It is an amazing concept—to be filled with all the fullness of God. Don't shy away from the implications of this truth. As believers we have been created to be containers of God. He desires to pour His life into ours and to fill us until we're full.

Let's think of this theologically for a moment. Colossians 2:9 tells us that in Christ the fullness of God dwells in bodily form. And when we come to Christ in faith, He comes to live in us. God in Christ is now reflected in us. That must lead to total moral reformation. Let's suppose you have a big jar of muddy water that you want to see become a jar of clear water. What's the quickest way to make the transformation? Take a garden hose and hook it up to an artesian spring filled with clear, cool, pure water. Now place the hose in the jar and turn on the water. As the clean water rushes in, it flushes out the muddy water. If you let the hose stay in the jar long enough, the muddy water will eventually be completely displaced by the clean water.

This is a parable of the Christian life. All of us are like jars of muddy water when we come to Christ. Some are muddier than others, but all of us are unclean when we find the Lord. It is the work of a lifetime to replace the muddy water of our sinful inclinations with the pure water of God's holy character. This is the answer to our entrenched bitterness, lust, greed, hate, envy, impatience, dishonesty, and unfaithfulness.

May Your love, O Lord, come into me and drive out my anger.

May Your holiness enter and drive out my greed.

May Your purity enter and drive out my lust.

May Your mercy fill my soul and wash away my envy.

When Your patience comes in, my impatience will vanish.

When Your grace fills me within, I can forgive.

All that Thou art, Lord Christ, with all Your shining beauty, come this moment and fill me. This is what Paul prays and envisions for every believer—to be filled with the fullness of God.

THE MAN WHO DENIED GOD

Being "filled to the measure of all the fullness of God" may sound impossible to someone who is conscious of the sin that stands between him and God. Sometimes our memory of past failure keeps us from believing what God has said. It may be that we have so grown accustomed to the "dirty water" of sin that we think it could never be made clean again. We wonder if God will take us back. Or will He turn us away? The answer is He will take us back, but we'll never know until we make that journey for ourselves. Several months ago I was the guest host on *Open Line,* the question-and-answer program heard nationally on the Moody Broadcasting Network. With about three minutes left in the program, I took one final call. As soon as I heard the man's voice, I knew he was distraught. He proceeded to tell a story unlike anything I have ever heard before. "I used to be a Christian, but my wife left me for another man. When she told me that she was leaving, I got angry and ripped up the Bible in front of her. Then I denied God in the name of the Trinity." His voice broke, and he started weeping. "I know it was wrong to do that, but I don't think God will ever take me back. What can I do?" I glanced at the clock and saw that we had about ninety seconds left in the program. It was a dilemma because this was the kind of call you wish you had a whole hour to discuss. But the seconds were ticking away, and I had to say something quickly.

"Sir, I don't have much time, so let me tell you this one thing. I know God loves you just the way you are, and He will take you back."

"But I ripped up the Bible in front of my wife."

"Sir, I know God loves you, and He will take you back."

"But I denied God in the name of the Trinity."

"God loves you, and He will take you back." The man wept openly as I said those words. Now we were down to the last thirty seconds. "We're almost out of time so I want you to listen carefully. Your broken heart tells me that God will take you back. The Lord never turns away a broken heart. When this program is over, I want you to get on your knees, put the Bible in front of you, tell the Lord you know the Bible is the Word of God, and ask Him to forgive you. And I want you to renounce your denial of faith. Tell the Lord that you know He is God, and ask the Lord Jesus to forgive you. Ask Him for a fresh start. If you do that, you will not be turned away." With that, our time ran out, and the program was over. I never heard from the man again. I don't know if he took my counsel or not. But I am sure that I told him the truth. No matter how great our sin may be, if we turn to the Lord, He will abundantly pardon. "Who is a God like you, who pardons sin and forgives the transgression of the remnant of his inheritance? You do not stay angry forever but delight to show mercy" (Micah 7:18).

This is all great, good news, but we must take it to heart. If we believe that in Jesus Christ dwells all the fullness of God (and we do), and if we believe Christ dwells in our hearts by faith (and we do), then we may believe that in our lives dwells the fullness of God, the beauty of God, the grace of God, the mercy of God, the holiness of God, the kindness of God, all that God is, God then may fill us and drive out the evil, lust, greed, impatience, unbelief, critical spirit, and the angry intolerance that holds us back. As the Holy Spirit changes us, the perfection of God is reflected in us. No matter what we may think, this is not impossible. It all goes back to the first request. This is the end result when we are strengthened inside by the Holy Spirit, even though it may seem far out of our reach.

THE ANSWER DEPENDS ON GOD

Unless God intervenes none of this can ever come to pass in our lives. How can we know that God will do it? It is such a big prayer! Paul gives us the answer in verses 20–21. The answer to this prayer is not up to us; it's up to God! That brings us to the magnificent doxology that concludes this prayer: **"Now to him who is able to do immeasurably more than all we ask or imagine, according to his power that is at work within us, to him be glory in the church and in Christ Jesus throughout all generations, for ever and ever! Amen"** (Ephesians 3:20–21).

Here is how verse 20 reads in the *New King James Version:* **"Now to Him who is able to do exceedingly abundantly above all that we ask or think, according to the power that works in us."** Both versions make clear that this prayer can be answered because God is able to answer it. Paul isn't saying, "I hope this will happen, but I'm not sure about it." We all live with a certain degree of inability: "Remember, Pastor Ray, you're only human." We live in a "hope so, maybe so, might be, and I'm not sure" kind of world. It's not a sign of weakness to admit your weakness when you really are weak. We can have assurance that God is able to do whatever it takes to answer this prayer. John Stott points out that there are seven stages in this great statement by the apostle Paul:

1. He is "able to do" because he is not idle or inactive or dead.
2. He can do "what we ask" because he hears us when we pray.
3. He can do "what we think" because he knows what we think before we think it.

4. He can do "all we ask or think" because he knows it all and can do it all.
5. He can do "more than we ask or think" because his plans are bigger than our plans.
6. He can do "much more" than we ask or think because there is no holding back with God.
7. He can do "exceedingly abundantly" beyond what we can imagine because he is the God of the superlative.[3]

Pay close attention to the phrase "exceedingly abundantly." Having two "-ly" adverbs back-to-back sounds strange to our ears. We may wonder if it is some sort of misprint, but it's not. The translators chose that odd formulation because it appears that Paul coined a Greek phrase that had never been used before. It has three parts. The first part means "above and beyond." The second part means "out of." The third part means "abundant." "Exceedingly abundantly" means infinitely above and beyond all human measurement. It's one thing to do what someone asks you to do. It's another thing to go beyond what he asks you to do. But it's something else to go infinitely beyond what he asks you to do. God's ability is "off the chart." It can't be measured. It's so great that it can't even be imagined. This verse is teaching us the exceeding, abundant, immeasurable, infinite ableness of God. There are no limits to what God can do. We can't even imagine what

God can do. His power is so great that we don't even know what we don't know.

"GOD CAN DO ANYTHING NOW"

It is not our prayers that mark His ability. *He can do far more than we can pray.* It is not our dreams and hopes that mark His ability. He can do things we can't even dream of. He is not limited by our prayers, our problems, our dreams, or even by our meager theories about who He is. This week I listened as a friend talked about what this text meant to him. After almost being destroyed by alcohol, drugs, and immorality, Christ saved him and utterly transformed his life, his marriage, his family, and his career. With profound gratitude, he thought about his own life in light of verse 20, and then he said, "God can do anything now." He's absolutely right.

And how does He do it? He does it "according to his power that is at work within us." It is "his power" but is power that is already at work "in us." The power to make this prayer come true is already at work in us. God's omnipotence is thus joined to my weakness. At the very point of my need—when I am weak, tired, fearful, doubting, discouraged, angry, upset, undone, and ready to give up and quit—at precisely that point, God's power is at work in me to give me what I need at that very moment. We may say this several ways:

Eternity joins time.

The infinite unites with my finiteness.

The transcendent touches the earthly.

The power of heaven is set loose on the earth.

The key to understanding God's power working in us is to remember the great promises of God that are given to every believer. We are already chosen . . . predestined . . . accepted . . . redeemed . . . sealed . . . saved . . . raised with Christ . . . united with Christ as members of His body . . . seated with Him in heaven . . . made citizens of heaven . . . called the children of God . . . and fellow heirs of all God has promised. If God has already done that for us, is there anything else we need that He won't provide for us? The answer is clear. God will give us what we need when we truly need it. It may not come early, and we may not experience all that we think we need, but God will never let His children down. He who knows what we truly need will see that we have it when we truly need it. If God is God, that must be true. Therefore, if we need power . . . endurance . . . patience . . . mercy . . . forgiveness . . . a way out of temptation . . . confidence . . . guidance . . . an answer to our prayers . . . a friend to help us . . . consolation . . . a clear conscience . . . inner peace . . . joy in hard times . . . a new idea . . . stamina . . . faith . . . hope . . . love . . . if we truly need those things (and we all need those things sooner or later—usually sooner), God will not hold back from us.

As Romans 8:32 puts it, "He who did not spare his own Son, but gave him up for us all—how will he not also, along with him, graciously give us all things?" Everything I need is available to me. Things I don't know about are available to me. Things I've never dreamed of are available to me.

Notice the arena of the promise. When this prayer is answered, God is greatly glorified "in the church" (v. 21). And God is greatly glorified when His power is displayed in the church. This means that God's power is available to all believers without distinction—young and old, rich and poor, male and female, new believers and seasoned saints, married and single, and of any ethnic origin and skin color. It also means that God's power is available to the church as a body. Thus, the church as a local congregation can pray this prayer and believe that God will answer it with a demonstration of His power.

The final part of verse 21 tells us that this promise of God's power will endure forever. Paul uses a very unusual expression to drive his point home. God's power will extend to every generation, and it will never come to an end. And what should this mean for us?

Teach this truth to your children because it is as good for the next generation as it is for this one. And learn it yourself because it is as true in bad times as it is in good times.

How should we apply this text? Let's start with your church. Suppose that the apostle Paul were the pastor of your local church. Do you think he would be impressed with what you have done? Would he look at the building, the musical instruments, the parking lot, the educational space, and say, "This is amazing!" I don't think so. Would he comment, "Wow! You've got PowerPoint!"? I doubt it. If Paul were your pastor, I think that every time he lifted his eyes to heaven he would hear God say, "I can do more in this church than you have yet asked or thought." That would lead him to pray for power and then step out in a new venture of faith for the Lord. When he looked again to heaven, he would hear God say, "Paul, I can do more!" So he would strike out again in a venture of faith, and God would say, "I can do more!" Each time he heard that, Paul would stretch himself out of his comfort zone and into the realm of impossibility. No matter what he did, the response of God would always be the same: "I can do more and more and more." We ought to consider our churches in light of this prayer. No matter how large or small our churches may be, I do not think we need to spend much time patting ourselves on the back for what we think we have accomplished. *We haven't even scratched the surface of what God can do in our churches.* God can always do more.

A Trinitarian Prayer

There is also personal application to be made.

When you are weak, pray to be strengthened on the inside. This is a prayer that God will always answer. And as you pray this prayer, ask God for these three things as a result: (1) that Christ might be at home in your heart, (2) for a growing comprehension of the love of Christ, and (3) for the fullness of God in your life.

Our greatest need is strength—so pray this prayer. Our greatest temptation is to make excuses or to seek better circumstances—so pray this prayer. As we pray this magnificent prayer, we will discover a Trinitarian answer. Look at Paul's words again.

All three persons of the Trinity are involved in this prayer:

> *"That the Holy Spirit might strengthen us."*
> *"That Christ might indwell us."*
> *"That God Himself might fill us."*

YOUR PRAYERS ARE TOO SMALL!

As I come to the end of this chapter, I want to emphasize the simplicity of our response. There is one crucial word in the text that I passed over earlier. In verse 17 Paul prays that **"Christ may dwell in your hearts through faith."** How simple this is. Pray in faith. God requires true, living faith and nothing else. Jesus comes in when faith opens the door. And He brings the fullness of God with him. Take the tiniest atom, infinitesimally small, far smaller than the naked eye can see. Take that atom and split it. You will release power beyond human calculation. Now take the simplest, smallest prayer offered in faith. That prayer will yield supernatural results in your life.

So, then, on the basis of this text: Pray boldly! Perhaps you've heard of J. B. Phillips' book *Your God Is Too Small.* Someone should write a book called *Your Prayers Are Too Small.* Pray big prayers to a big God. "Open wide your mouth and I will fill it," says the Lord (Psalm 81:10). Pray for that which only God can answer.

> *Thou art coming to a King*
> *Large petitions with Thee bring*
> *For his grace and power are such*
> *None can ever ask too much.*

And while you are praying, pray that God will be glorified in the answer to your prayers. This means that God's reality will be so clearly demonstrated that His reputation is enhanced in the world.

Is God Able?

At the end of the day there is one final question our fearful hearts may ask. You may wonder, "Is God able to help me?" No matter how many verses you read, inner fear and deep doubt can erase any spark of hope. The question is real: Is God able? If we believe the Bible, the answer must be yes.

Is there enough sunlight to light your living room?
Is there enough water in the ocean to fill a thimble?

All too often our focus is on our problems when it ought to be on God. If you look at your own weakness, the logical conclusion will be discouragement, doubt, and frustration. But if you focus on His unlimited power, you will find faith and hope in spite of your circumstances. How weak we are. How Lilliputian our strength.

Consider God. Think on Him. "Ponder anew what the Almighty can do, if with his love he befriend you." How strong God is! Who knows what He will do? God has infinite ways of helping us.

He is able to strengthen us when we are weak.
He is able to answer far more than we ask.
He is able to hear the faintest cry.
He is able to lift our burdens in the time of crisis.
He is able to guide us when we have lost our way.

But what if you are in a crisis situation even as you read these words? What if you are in a "fiery furnace" at this moment? Remember this: He brought you into it,

He will be with you in it, and when His purposes are accomplished, He will lead you out of it. And you'll be surprised how He does it. When I was growing up in northwest Alabama, my father would sometimes take us to visit the farm where he grew up outside of Oxford, Mississippi. The drive took a little over two hours, and we would pass through a number of small towns on the way—Belgreen, Red Bay, Fulton, Tupelo, and New Albany. My brothers and I would say, "Are we there yet?" and Dad would answer, "No, not yet." Eventually we would fall asleep, and when we woke up, we were there! It seemed like magic to us, but our father knew the way because he had traveled it many times. He knew all along how to get there and wasn't going to make a mistake.

In the same way, our heavenly Father knows the way we should go. He knows how to lead us safely on the journey from earth to heaven. And even when we think we've taken a wrong turn or perhaps are going in circles, our Father knows what He is doing. And one day we'll open our eyes in wonder and amazement and say, "Wow! How did we end up here?"

How can we be sure of that? Because "God is able." What God is that? The God of Abraham, Isaac, and Jacob. The God of Moses. The God of Israel. The God and Father of our Lord Jesus Christ. The God who spoke a thousand million galaxies into being. The God who has numbered the grains of sand. The God who knows the number of hairs on your head. The God who sees the sparrow when it falls. The God who holds the universe in His hands. *That God, the almighty, all-powerful, all-knowing, ever-present God of the universe—He will direct your paths.* If God has said He will lead you, then why are you fearful? If God has said He will take up your cause, then why are you worried about tomorrow?

> No evil can baffle you if He leads the way.
> No enemy can stop you if He leads the way.
> No opposition can derail you if He leads the way.
> No obstacle can forever stand against you if He leads the way.

No one can say for sure how He will do it. There are thousands of ways in which God leads His children. He leads us through delays, detours, miracles, the advice of friends, unexpected opportunities, suddenly closed doors, answered prayer, unanswered prayer, inner impressions, and a still small voice. You don't see how he leads you this side of heaven. On this side you see the problems. But when you know God, He leads you step-by-step. You will look back and say, "I don't know how I got from there to here, but I do know this: Jesus led me all the way."

So we marvel at the richness of an amazing prayer tied to an amazing promise. It is an impossible prayer made possible because "God is able" to do "exceedingly abundantly" beyond all we could ask or think. God wants us to pray, He invites us to pray, and He waits for us to call upon Him. He is able to hear us and to answer us. If we do our part and pray, God does not fail to do His.

Heavenly Father, thank You that Your provision is far greater than my need. I come in Jesus' name, deeply conscious of my weakness. Strengthen me by Your power on the inside so that I might walk the path You have set for me. May my life be a fitting dwelling place for the Lord Jesus, and may I continue to grow in His love. Grant me fresh faith to believe in You. Teach me to pray big prayers that You might be honored in a big way in my life. Thank You that what You have already done is only the beginning. Be glorified in me, in my family, and in my church—today, tomorrow, and forever! Through Jesus Christ our Lord, Amen.

2 THESSALONIANS 1:11—12

✜

*"With this in mind, we constantly pray for you,
that our God may count you worthy of his calling,
and that by his power he may fulfill every good purpose of yours and every act prompted by your faith.
We pray this so that the name of our Lord Jesus may
be glorified in you, and you in him, according to
the grace of our God and the Lord Jesus Christ."*

5

HANGING TOUGH FOR JESUS

In order to properly understand this prayer, we need to back up a few verses so we can understand the context properly: "Therefore, among God's churches we boast about your perseverance and faith in all the persecutions and trials you are enduring. All this is evidence that God's judgment is right, and as a result you will be counted worthy of the kingdom of God, for which you are suffering" (2 Thessalonians 1:4–5). Note the words Paul uses when he addresses the Thessalonians: "persecutions," "trials," and "suffering." This prayer is different from the ones we have considered previously, because the people Paul was praying for were in a desperate situation.

It's never been easy to be a Christian, but in some parts of the world it is extremely difficult and even dangerous. Kurdish convert Ziwar Mohammed Ismaeel was shot and killed in a city in northern Iraq.[1] When Ismaeel became a Christian, his family asked the leader of the local mosque what to do since he had left the Muslim faith. The mullah declared him an apostate and recommended that he be killed. Some of his relatives captured him and took him out to a remote place, where they gave him the choice of either renouncing his faith in Christ or being killed. His friends managed to rescue him and sent him into hiding. But Ismaeel refused to stay there very long because he did not want to show fear. "With Jesus on my side, I have nothing to fear," he declared. "I have to go back to my family and tell them that even when they kill me, I will never deny Christ."

He made his living as a taxi driver. On the morning of February 17, 2003, he was waiting in a line of taxis at the train station for his turn to receive passengers. A stranger approached and began talking with him. Fellow taxi drivers said that Ismaeel offered a cup of tea to the man, who then began to demand loudly that Ismaeel deny his faith in Christ and come back to Islam. When Ismaeel refused, saying he could not stop believing in Christ, the stranger asked him to step aside and talk privately with him. Just seconds later, eyewitnesses said, the man pulled out a machine gun and started shooting point-blank at Ismaeel. Twenty-eight bullets were pumped into his body, killing Ismaeel on the spot. When the police captured his killer, the man claimed be fulfilling the will of Allah and said, "I don't feel guilty for doing it." He was said to be a member of the Islamic Union who had spent two years in Afghanistan. A friend who knew Ismaeel said, "He was always exhorting other Christians to be bold, to not be afraid." He left behind a wife and five children.

GOD'S JUDGMENT IS RIGHT

And Paul said, "I boast everywhere I go about your faith and your perseverance." Then he says something that sounds a bit strange, if you think about it. "This is evidence that God's judgment is right." What does he mean, God's judgment is right? How can it be right for a woman to become a widow because her husband was a Christian? How does the death of a persecuted Christian prove that God's judgment is right? By itself, it doesn't prove anything. Persecution is a terrible reality for millions of believers around the world, but that's not exactly what Paul is referring to. He's not saying, "Everywhere I go I boast about your persecution," as if that by itself was a good thing. He's not praising evildoers because they are somehow doing Christians a favor by persecuting them.

To say that would be to turn morality upside down and virtually say that evil has somehow become good. That can't be right. Evil is always evil.

Paul's boast was not in their persecution but in their perseverance and in their faith. The Greek word for perseverance is very important. It literally means to "remain under" something. In this context it describes a person who will not be swayed from his loyalty to Christ even by the greatest trials and sufferings. Perseverance is not merely enduring trials with gritted teeth, but patiently waiting with radiant hope for the dawn of a better day.

Then Paul adds something else in verse 5. By your suffering, God is making you "worthy" of the kingdom. Another way to say it is, "God is making you fit for heaven." There are two things we can remind ourselves of when we go through hard times because of our faith. First, *the Lord notices our sufferings.* He who sees the sparrow when it falls to the ground, keeps a watchful eye on His suffering children. Just as a parent takes special care of a child who is ill, the Lord gives special attention to His children who bear reproach for His sake. Second, *our sufferings have an eternal purpose.* They are not random acts of fate. When Mr. Ismaeel went to his taxi stand, the Lord went with him. And when his assailant pumped twenty-eight bullets into his body, the Lord stood by his side. And when he died, the Lord was there to welcome him home to heaven. Whatever else we may say about it, we must confess that our Lord makes no mistakes, even though many things in this life have no explanation.

GOD NEVER SAYS "OOPS!"

On the day the war in Iraq started, I spoke to the older students at Oak Park Christian Academy. I could see fear etched on their faces. I told them that I wished I could promise them that war would not come, but I couldn't promise it because war might come. And I told them that I wished I could promise them that terrorists would never strike the United States again, but I couldn't say that because it might happen eventually. The future is uncertain for all of us. I told the students that the Bible says "fear not" over 300 times. God's word to us today and tomorrow is, "Fear not!" When the troops march and the bombs fall, His word is the same, "Fear not." His word for the day after tomorrow is "Fear not." Finally, I told the children to remember two things: First, the Lord is always with us no matter what happens. Second, the Lord makes no mistakes no matter how scary life may seem.

When asked by her mother what she learned in Sunday school, a little girl answered, "I learned that God never says, 'Oops!'" In the same way, God did not say "Oops!" when the war started in Iraq that night. There are no surprises with God. Even our trials somehow fit into His plan for us.

Paul's prayer for the suffering believers in Thessalonica comes in verses 11–12. As he does in other places, he packs a great deal into just a few phrases. This is a wartime prayer. You could summarize it this way: "I am praying for you, that you will hang tough for Jesus no matter how hard it gets."

TWO REQUESTS

That You Might Be Living Proof

"With this in mind, we constantly pray for you, that our God may count you worthy of his calling" (2 Thessalonians 1:11a). Paul has already said in verse 5 that the Thessalonians' steady faith under pressure was proof that God was making them worthy of the kingdom. Now he prays that God will keep doing what He's already started to do. Note once again that Paul doesn't say, "I pray that your trials might go away." He doesn't say, "I am praying that your persecution would soon come to an end." Those are legitimate requests, but that's not how Paul prays. In the spiritual realm there are no shortcuts to maturity. No pain, no gain. *Paul understood the evangelistic value of a steadfast faith.* "Lord, make my brothers and sisters living proof so that the whole world will know what You can do through believers who can take the heat and not give up." The motto of the Marine Corps is "Semper Fidelis," which means "always faithful." Often it is shortened to "Semper Fi." That should be our motto as well: Semper Fi—always faithful to the Lord, our calling, and our family! *When you know where you are going, you can be "always faithful" to the very end.*

Hugh Latimer was a Protestant preacher in England in the 1500s. When Queen Mary ("Bloody Mary") came to the throne, she attempted to return England to the Roman Catholic Church. Latimer protested and was thrown into jail along with his friend Nicholas Ridley. Convicted of heresy, they were sentenced to be burned at the stake. The sentence was carried out on October 16, 1555. As they approached the stake, Ridley drew back in fear. Latimer comforted his friend with words that have echoed across the generations: "Be of good cheer, Master Ridley, and play the man, for we shall this day light such a candle in England as I trust by God's grace shall never be put out." And so they did light a candle for God by their fiery ordeal. They were living proof to the very end. Semper Fi—always faithful to the Lord.

That You Might Have God-centered Goals

"And that by his power he may fulfill every good purpose of yours and every act prompted by your faith" (2 Thessalonians 1:11b). Translators have a hard time with this verse because it's not totally clear what Paul is saying. Let me give you two other versions of this request:

1. We "pray that he will fill your good ideas and acts of faith with his own energy so that it all amounts to something" (THE MESSAGE).
2. "We pray for God's power to help you do all the good things that you hope to do and that your faith makes you want to do" (CEV).

We all have ideas, but not every idea is a good idea. Not every dream is a good dream, and not every goal is a worthy goal. *There are dreams and ideas that are good and worthy because they come from God.* Paul is saying, "I'm praying that you won't waste your life on things that don't matter. I don't want to see you come to the end and say, 'I blew it.' So I'm praying that you will figure out what really matters in life, and then you will have the faith to go and do it." Unless the Lord builds the house, those who build it labor in vain (Psalm 127).

Five weeks after the terrorist attack on September 11, 2001, I stood with a group of four men at Ground Zero in Manhattan looking at the ruins of the World Trade Center. We had traveled twenty-four hundred miles through eleven states in one hundred hours to deliver copies of the book *An Anchor for the Soul* to Christian ministries in New York City. We left Oak Park, Illinois, on Sunday afternoon and drove straight through to High Point, North Carolina, where we picked up copies of the book from the Prison Fellowship warehouse. On Monday night we visited the Pentagon and stood close to where the plane crashed into the building. Later that night we stood in front of the White House and prayed for the president and for the nation. On Wednesday we were in New York City where we led a church service in the Bronx, and on Thursday we drove back to Oak Park. At the end of our worship service in the Bronx, I talked with a young firefighter from Yonkers named Scott. His company had been called to the World Trade Center about 1:30 A.M. on September 12. Everything was still in chaos. Other buildings were about to collapse. The scene sounded like something out of *Dante's Inferno.* As he recounted the story, Scott said that what he experienced there caused him to get serious about his Christian faith.

A few days later someone asked what I learned from our visit to Ground Zero. I replied that one fact keeps pounding away in my brain. The words of 1 John 2:17 come through loud and clear: "The world is passing away along with its desires, but whoever does the will of God abides forever" (ESV). As I stood just a few feet from the twisted, smoking ruins of the World Trade Center, I kept thinking, "This is what the world comes to sooner or later. Everything built by man can be destroyed by man. These things do not last forever."

September 11 ought to be a wake-up call for all of us to reconsider our personal priorities. What are you living for? "For what does it profit a man to gain the whole world and forfeit his life?" (Mark 8:36, ESV). There is a message here for all of us if we will heed it: "Find out what matters in life. And then go and do it!" Not everything matters. Not everything is truly as important as we think it is.

That's where this prayer becomes so powerful. When you pray for others, pray that they will pursue godly goals instead of worldly goals, and that they will be given strength to fulfill all that God has for them to do. By the way, this is a powerful prayer for parents to pray for their children. Ask the Lord to give them godly goals. Pray that your children will dream big dreams for God and have the energetic faith to see them come to pass.

TWO RESULTS

Christ is glorified in us.

"We pray this so that the name of our Lord Jesus may be glorified in you" (2 Thessalonians 1:12a). To glorify the name of Christ means to enhance His reputation in the world. For Ziwar Mohammed Ismaeel, glorifying Christ meant being faithful to the point of death. For all of us, it means living so that others know that we know Jesus and are not ashamed of Him. We have a tremendous evangelistic opportunity during hard times if we will respond with grace and dignity. *The world watches closely to see if our religion works as well in the darkness as it does in the sunlight.* Many people have been converted not by a sermon but by the testimony of God's grace shining through the pain a believer endures.

So when you pray, ask God to make you strong in your weak places so that you will be like the house built on the rock. Though the rains come down and the floodwaters rise, your house will stand firm because it is built on a solid foundation (Matthew 7:24–27).

Two weeks ago my friend Bruce Thorn called to say hello. Bruce and I grew up together in Alabama and have been friends for almost forty years. Every time he calls me, he shares something that comes right from the heart of God. This time he started talking about smoke and mirrors. To most of us, that phrase brings to mind magicians such as Penn & Teller who use smoke and mirrors to conceal reality. But Bruce said that God uses smoke and mirrors to reveal the truth. The "smoke" is like the cloudy pillar that led the children of Israel through the wilderness. And the "mirror" is like the mirror referred to in 1 Corinthians 13 that describes the day when we will all stand before the Lord. Now we see things dimly, and we can conceal things from each other. But when we stand before the Lord, all will be revealed, and the total truth about each one of us will be fully known. Bruce said that lots of people prefer smoke and mirrors because they don't want to know the truth about themselves. They would rather cover up than confront their flaws. The prayer here is, "Lord, give me a strong heart and a good foundation so that I can survive hard times with my faith intact so that those who know me will know that I know You."

We are glorified in him.

"And you in him" (2 Thessalonians 1:12b). I thought about this little phrase all week long, but it wasn't until late last night that I finally got my hands around it. It's like playing on Michael Jordan's team. In fact, it's as if you are standing in a vast crowd of people and MJ looks at you and says, "I want you on my team."

"But I don't even know how to play basketball," you reply.

"Don't worry about it," Michael says. "Just pass the ball to me, and I'll do the rest." So that's what you do. You go out on the basketball court in front of thousands of cheering fans with millions of people watching on TV. It's a heady experience, but then you remember that they aren't cheering for you. They don't even know who you are. But it doesn't matter. You're on Michael Jordan's team. When the game starts, someone passes you the ball. You don't even take a step. You just look for MJ and throw the ball to him. He then does one of those patented head fake, double-pump, around the back, through the legs, 360-degree rotation, tomahawk slam-dunks. The crowd goes wild. He gets the points, and you get an assist. As you go back down the court, he grins at you and says, "Nice pass." And that's how it is all game long. You get the ball and pass it to Michael. That's all you ever do. But that's enough because he's the greatest there ever was. And guess what? Your team ends up winning the game in double overtime. Afterward the reporters crowd around Michael to ask him questions. No one seems to know you were even in the game. But then you hear Michael Jordan say your name. He's telling the reporters he couldn't have done it without you. You smile even though you know that he didn't need you; anyone could have passed the ball to him. But he chose you, and you did it. Because of your passing and MJ's greatness, you won the game. Michael was the hero, but you share in his victory because you were on his team.

As wonderful as that fantasy might be for a basketball fan, something much greater is in store for us. We're on Jesus' team. He chose us, and He made us starters. We can't do much, and without Him, we can't do anything at all. The game is long and hard, and sometimes it seems like we're going to lose because the other team is mean and vicious, and they cheat all the time. But in the end Team Jesus comes out on top because the captain of our team is the King of kings and Lord of lords. He's the greatest there ever was, and He's the greatest there ever will be. We're joined with Him by faith so that when He wins, we win. That's what it means to be glorified in Him. We're not much, but the glory that comes to Him comes also to us because He looks at us and says with a smile, "Nice pass," even though we know He could have done it without us. We share in His glory because we are on His team. That's the final reward for hanging tough for Jesus.

When you stand strong under pressure, four things happen:

1. You are living proof of God's power.
2. You accomplish God's goals for your life.
3. You glorify Christ with your life.
4. You share in His ultimate victory.

What a wonderful way to live. What a wonderful way to pray. Here's the best argument I know for hanging tough in hard times and dreaming big dreams for God. We're all going to die someday. Therefore, the only question is whether you're going to die playing it safe or risking it all for the Lord. I don't want to die until I'm dead. I want to live until the very last moment, fully invested for Jesus Christ and for His kingdom. I want to be doing everything I can to advance His cause in the world and take risks on the basis of kingdom principles. I don't want to waste my few years on this planet hoarding my resources so I can have earthly security. That's not what the life of faith is about.

One additional point. If you decide to live on the edge, you may not be completely successful. Maybe things will work out for you, maybe they won't. If you decide to become someone who takes risks for Jesus Christ, will you see success in all that you do? Probably not. Most of the men and women in the Bible who took great risks saw only partial success for their efforts. Abraham made it to the Promised Land but lived his whole life in tents. Moses led his people to the Jordan River but could go no farther. Joshua conquered the land, but not all the enemies were defeated. So it goes for those who live by faith.

Our great calling is to find out what God is doing in the world and then to fling ourselves wholeheartedly into His cause. Let me make that more specific. At some point you must put down this book and go back to daily life. Go back to your world, your home, your business, your neighborhood, your classroom, your club, your family, your church, your town, your city, your state, and your nation and find out what God is doing there. Then go do it with Him. Throw yourself without hesitation into God's work in your world. And then get ready for the time of your life. That's God's call to all of us. If we win, we win. If we lose, we lose.

But in the end, the only losers will be those who held themselves back from teaming up with God.

ALL BY GRACE, ALL THE TIME

Are you experiencing hard times right now? Are you perplexed by some persecution you're going through or wiped out with some worry? God's word to you is clear: Stand firm. Stay the course. Don't despair. Don't give up. One day God will make everything right. Our responsibility is to hang tough for Jesus.

There is one final phrase that I don't want us to miss. It tells us how all this is possible: **"According to the grace of our God and the Lord Jesus Christ"** (2 Thessalonians 1:12c). It's all by grace, all the time. Everything in the Christian life is by grace. We are saved by grace, we live by grace, we hang tough by grace, we die by grace, and we go to heaven by grace.

If you truly know Jesus Christ, you can hang tough and live without fear because you know whatever comes, you'll be all right. One day I got a call that Frank Catrambone had been taken to a local hospital with serious blood clots in his lungs and in one of the vessels leading to his heart. His situation was extremely critical. By the time I got to the Intensive Care Unit, he had been given some sort of powerful clot-dissolving drug that was dangerous because it could possibly cause a stroke. When I saw Frank (who is over eighty years old), he shook my hand and said, "Pastor, it's good to see you."

When I asked him how he was doing, he smiled through his oxygen mask and said, "I have the best physician in the world. His name is Jesus Christ." I thought, "How do you stop a man like that?" You can't. He's placed his life in the hands of the Great Physician, and that's why he can face whatever comes with a smile.

In 1981 when President Ronald Reagan was nearly assassinated, his pastor from California came to see him in the hospital in Washington, D.C. Pastor Don Moomaw took the president's hand and asked him, "How is it with you and the Lord?"

"Everything is fine with me and the Lord," replied Mr. Reagan.

"How do you know?"

The answer was simple and profound: "I have a Savior."

That's the difference that Jesus Christ makes. When you have a Savior, you can face your own death with courage and grace. Do you have a Savior? If you don't, or if you aren't sure, I urge you to place your life in the hands of Jesus Christ right now. Trust Him as Lord and Savior. Ask Him to take away your sins and to give you new life. Come to Christ, and your life will never be the same again.

Heavenly Father, Your kingdom will last long after this world has crumbled to the dust. Help me to live today for the things that will last forever. Thank You that my hardest trials are part of Your plan. Make me living proof of Your power so that those who know me will know that I know You. May I never be ashamed to say, "I believe in Jesus." In His name, Amen.

2 THESSALONIANS 2:13—17

✛

"But we ought always to thank God for you, brothers loved by the Lord, because from the beginning God chose you to be saved through the sanctifying work of the Spirit and through belief in the truth. He called you to this through our gospel, that you might share in the glory of our Lord Jesus Christ. So then, brothers, stand firm and hold to the teachings we passed on to you, whether by word of mouth or by letter. May our Lord Jesus Christ himself and God our Father, who loved us and by his grace gave us eternal encouragement and good hope, encourage your hearts and strengthen you in every good deed and word."

6

STRENGTH FOR THE JOURNEY

Not long ago I received a letter from Pat Williams, Executive Vice President of the professional basketball team, the Orlando Magic. Although I had never met Mr. Williams, I knew he was a brilliant sports executive and also a devoted Christian. He wrote to say that he was working on a book about the life of Christ and wondered if I had any thoughts that might be helpful. I jotted down a page or two of ideas and sent them to him by e-mail. A few months later I received a copy of his book, *How to Be Like Jesus: Lessons on Following in His Footsteps.*[1] As I browsed through it, I came to a chapter called "How to Endure Like Jesus." There was a quote from German theologian Otto Dibelius, a leader of the anti-Nazi resistance movement in World War Two: "God does not lead his children around hardship, but leads them straight through hardship. But he leads! And amidst the hardship, he is nearer to them than ever before." That's a striking way to put it. Not around hardship but straight through it.

Pat Williams then addresses the issue of endurance head-on: "If we want to be like Jesus, we must endure like Jesus. We need to persevere under pressure like Jesus did . . . If it hasn't happened already, a time will come when you must endure like Jesus . . . No one in history deserved to be more honored and respected than Jesus of Nazareth. Yet he was treated with contempt and put to death. If we endure like Jesus, our own battle scars will be the righteous and beautiful wounds of those who have taken a courageous stand against evil. Our wounds will be like his."

Life is a journey for all of us, and that journey is not always easy. There are hard days and difficult nights, and sometimes there are weeks and months and years where the road seems to lead from one hardship to another. If we live long enough, we'll have plenty of chances to get the battle scars Pat Williams talks about. No one gets a free ride, and no one is exempt from the troubles of the world.

A woman e-mailed the news that she was going in for surgery. When I saw her a week later in church, she seemed to be doing well, but she said the doctor had sent some tissue samples to a lab for closer examination to find out if they were malignant. A few days later she got the news that she had cancer in two places in her body. A second e-mail told of her plans to treat the cancer. She added this sentence: "I look forward to how God will glorify Himself in this." I glean two important truths from her godly response to her cancer: First, it is not wrong to pray for healing or to seek competent medical help. Medicine and faith are allies, not enemies. Second, our greatest need is *always* for wisdom from God so that we will understand how His plan is working out in our trials. When I wrote her back, I told her what she already knew—that even the cancer would be used by the Lord for her good and for His glory, and that there would likely be some moments when the "good" and the "glory" were not easy to see. But I liked her phrase "I look forward" because it suggests to me a runner leaning into the tape at the finish line. Sometimes the trials of life cause us to "lean back" or to "fall away" altogether. It is a great advance in the spiritual life to "look forward" with anticipation to what God will accomplish in us even through times of adversity. He intends to glorify Himself in our trials, and He will do it, if we will trust Him.

Sometimes when we are discouraged, we can feel

like giving up and walking away from the Lord. We're not the first generation to feel like that. This passage ends with a prayer by Paul for the young congregation at Thessalonica. It helps to remember that these new believers were just recently rescued from paganism. Now they were under intense pressure to leave Jesus and go back to their old life. That's why Paul prays in verses 16–17 that they would be encouraged and stabilized by the Lord. In order to grasp the full impact of his prayer, we need to start at verse 13. There we will find a message of encouragement that speaks to us in the 21st century.

A DOCTRINE WE NEED TO BELIEVE

"But we ought always to thank God for you, brothers loved by the Lord, because from the beginning God chose you to be saved through the sanctifying work of the Spirit and through belief in the truth. He called you to this through our gospel, that you might share in the glory of our Lord Jesus Christ" (2 Thessalonians 2:13–14).

The whole system of Christian theology can be found in these verses. Everything we believe is here in tightly compressed fashion. The key phrase is "God chose you to be saved." That speaks of the sovereign grace of God in salvation. Did you know God chose you to be saved? If He had not chosen you, you would never have been saved at all. Sometimes we speak of "finding" the Lord, but if He had not found us first, we would never have found Him at all. Salvation begins with God—not with us. He chooses us—and then we believe. In putting the matter that way, I simply mean to declare that salvation is all by grace, all of God, all the time. One Sunday when I was preaching on this text, I met with some men to pray in my office. One of them asked, "You're not going to talk about predestination today, are you?"

I laughed and said, "You bet I am." It's in the text so I can't ignore it or pretend that it's not there. Many years ago, when I was growing up in Alabama, my friend David Neal and I used to sit on his porch late at night and talk about the Bible. We decided that someday we were going to write a twenty-volume masterwork called *Why We're Confused About Predestination*. I saw David a few weeks ago, and that brought our late-night theology sessions back to my mind. Thirty-five years have come and gone since those mostly carefree days. I know a great deal more than I knew back then, but there is still much that I do not understand. At this point I wouldn't say that I am confused about predestination. I would use the word "mystery" to describe the relationship between human responsibility and divine sovereignty. Some things that God understands are simply not fully understandable to us. After all, the first rule of the spiritual life informs us that "He's God and we're not."

And so when Paul says, "God chose us for salvation," I am happy to believe it just as it is written. But that doesn't mean I can fully explain every nuance of how our unforced choices fit into God's sovereign plan for the universe. But they do. I believe that God arranges the circumstances of life (and the movements of the heart) to bring us to the place where we have no other choice but to freely choose to trust in Christ for salvation. To some that will seem like a contradiction, to others it will seem like a simple statement of biblical truth. Is there a mystery here? Yes, of course, and I would much prefer a theology with some mystery in it to a theology that claimed to fully explain the mind of God. *When it comes to salvation, we bring the sin that makes salvation necessary, and God brings everything else.* Yet we are not robots or puppets on a string, and when we come to Christ, we do not come conscious of any compulsion. We come by faith because we want to come. And in our coming, we discover later that God was drawing us to Himself all along by the power of the Holy Spirit. If you are troubled by this, or wonder how it could be, just remember that you are on the right track when your view of salvation gives all the glory to God. Magnify the Lord as Savior, give Him the credit, and you will be moving in the right direction.

FROM ETERNITY TO ETERNITY

These three verses lay out the five stages or steps in our salvation in the broadest possible sense:

1. **You were loved (v. 13).** Salvation springs from the heart of God who loved us and gave His Son for us. The message of the gospel is always "God loves you. God loves you. God loves you." And this should be the church's message as well.

2. **You were chosen (v. 13).** This is sovereign grace, divine choice, divine election, and pre-destination. This means that when it comes to salvation, God always makes the first move, and if He didn't make the first move, we would never make any move at all.

3. **You were called (v. 14).** The "sanctifying work of the Spirit" refers to the wooing of the Holy Spirit whereby He creates in the heart of the lost sinner a conviction of sin and a desire to come to Christ for salvation. Without this work of the Spirit, no one would ever come to Christ.

4. **You believed the gospel (vv. 14–15).** This is where our responsibility comes into play. We still must believe the gospel. No one goes to heaven apart from the work of Christ on the cross.

5. **You share in Christ's glory (v. 14).** This is the final step in our salvation. And it is a step still in the future. One day we will be with the Lord in heaven, and we will share in His great victory.

In a sense, this is the whole sweep of salvation from "eternity to eternity." There is great comfort in seeing things from this perspective. It tells us that God has a purpose in history. He's not just "making it up" as He goes along. Everything in the universe plays a part in the outworking of God's plan. This ought to give us enormous confidence as we face the uncertainties of day-to-day life. If you believe that everything in your life is a hit-and-miss affair that happens by chance, then you will be a prisoner to your circumstances. You'll be up when things are good, and you'll be down when things are bad. How wonderful it is to rest in the knowledge that our God is working out His plan for us in everything that happens to us—the good and the bad, the positive and the negative, the happy and the sad.

By the way, don't let this doctrine trouble you about who can or can't be saved. God desires that all should come to repentance (2 Peter 3:9). God loves the whole world (John 3:16). The gospel is to be preached to every nation (Matthew 29:19–20). There is no one who wants to be saved who cannot be saved! Rest assured in these truths. *No one will be in hell by accident. No one will be in hell who truly ought to be in heaven.* No one will be in hell who can legitimately say, "I wanted to be saved, but God would not save me." Such a thing simply cannot happen. If you have the desire to know God, you can be confident that He gave that longing to you. God is always the initiator in salvation. God calls, we respond. God calls, we believe. God calls, we come to Christ. He sent His Son to die for us that we could be united to Him forever. He sent His Spirit to draw us. And He gave us His Word so we would know the truth. And He even gives us faith to believe the gospel. And when the church goes out to preach the gospel, the Lord goes with us so we don't go in our own power. Salvation is of the Lord!

DEATH TODAY, GLORY TOMORROW

The very best part of this is the final step in the process—sharing in His glory in the life to come. That hasn't happened yet. Today death still reigns on planet Earth. Turn on the TV and you hear about war and killing and bloodshed. Death reigns because death has not yet been destroyed. If you doubt that, check out the obituaries in the newspaper. There are lots of people going into the cemeteries—not many coming out. If you are waiting for a resurrection at the cemetery, you may have to wait a long time. Death is everywhere. It is the one appointment no one can postpone. I've been thinking about this quite a bit since my mother died a few months ago. Someone said that it must have been hard for me to speak at her graveside service, but it wasn't hard at all. It was a tremendous honor to do that for my mother. Near the end of my message, I turned to face my mom's casket and the place where my father was buried right next to her. I ended by saying, "Rest well, Dad. Rest well, Mom. We will see you again." Is that just wishful thinking? Is there any basis for believing that we will ever see our loved ones again? Let the apostle Paul answer that question:

"We believe that Jesus died and rose again and so we believe that God will bring with Jesus those who have fallen asleep in him. According to the Lord's own word, we tell you that we who are still alive, who are left till the coming of the Lord, will certainly not precede those who have fallen asleep. For the Lord himself will come down from heaven, with a loud command, with the voice of the archangel and with the trumpet call of God, and the dead in Christ will rise first. After that, we who are still alive and are left will be caught up together with them in the clouds to meet the Lord in the air. And so we will be with the Lord forever" (1 Thessalonians 4:14–17).

Everything hinges on the first phrase: "We believe that Jesus died and rose again." In the King James Version, the translators added a word. "*If* we believe that Jesus died and rose again . . ." The *New Living Translation* says, "Since we believe." I think that both versions are correct. We do believe, and since we believe, we are banking on these things being true. If we don't believe, then we have no certainty at all. *Everything hinges on what happened on Easter Sunday morning two thousand years ago.* Many years ago I was asked to perform a graveside service for a man I barely knew. I was young and inexperienced and wanted to say a few words of comfort. I fumbled my way through the ceremony and came to the closing prayer. When I got to the part about the resurrection of the dead, the words stuck in my throat. I could barely finish my prayer. I went back home, frustrated and embarrassed. What had gone wrong? Then it hit me. I wasn't sure I believed in the resurrection of the dead. Up until then, it had all been theoretical. But now that I had come face-to-face with death, my brave words seemed so hollow.

Out of that experience I began to pray, and it seemed as if God said to me, "Son, you're looking in the wrong place." There is indeed a grave that's empty, but it's over on the other side of the world, outside Jerusalem, carved into a mountainside. That tomb is empty, and it's been empty for two thousand years.

Several years ago I visited the Holy Land for the first time. During our visit to Jerusalem, we spent an hour at the Garden Tomb, the spot believed by many to be the actual burial place of Jesus. It is located next to Gordon's Calvary, that strange rock outcropping that appears to be worn into the shape of a skull. We know it was used as a burial site in Jesus' day. Many believe it was the spot of the crucifixion. The Garden Tomb is located about one hundred yards from Gordon's Calvary and is in fact the spot of a beautiful garden built over an ancient Roman aqueduct. To your left as you enter is a typical first-century tomb dug into the hillside. A trench in front of the opening was apparently designed for the massive stone that once covered the entrance.

NO BODY THERE

Because the opening is very small, I had to duck to go inside. You see nothing until your eyes adjust to the darkness. Then you can easily make out the two chambers. Visitors stand in the mourners' chamber. A wrought iron fence protects the chamber where the body was laid. You soon notice that the burial chamber was originally designed for two bodies. However, one ledge was never finished for some reason. The other one was. It appears to be designed for a person slightly less than six feet tall.

As I looked around the burial chamber, I could see faint markings left by Christian pilgrims from earlier centuries. After a few seconds another thought entered my mind. *There was no body to be found in this tomb.* Whoever was buried there evidently left a long time ago. The Garden Tomb is empty!

As you exit back into the sunlight, your eyes fasten upon a wooden sign: "Why seek ye the living among the dead? He is not here, for he is risen, as he said."

We look at our loved ones dying and wonder if the resurrection can be true. But that's backward. God says, "Look what I did for My Son. Will I do any less for those who put their trust in Him?" Put simply: We do not believe in the resurrection of the dead because of anything we can see with our eyes; everything we see argues against it. People die all the time. There hasn't been a resurrection in a long, long time. But that doesn't matter. We believe in the resurrection of the saints because we believe in the resurrection of Jesus. "For if we believe that Jesus died and rose again and so we believe that God will bring with Jesus those who have fallen asleep in him" (1 Thessalonians 4:14).

QUESTION TIME WITH THE SPARKS

Each year I am invited to speak to the children in our AWANA "Sparks" program (K–2nd grade) for a special "Ask Pastor Ray" night where the kids try to stump me with Bible questions. It seems to get easier to stump me as the years go by. On my most recent visit, I took questions from over one hundred very excited children. The very first question was, "How many letters are in the Bible?" Then, "How many words are in the Bible?" Then, "How many sentences are in the Bible?" Hmm. I was 0 for 3 and fading fast. Then someone wanted to know, "How tall was Jesus?" Then, "Who is taller—you or Jesus?" Then, "Is Jesus taller than God?" (There were a few theological problems with that question.) And on it went. One boy wanted to know, "How many clouds are there?"

"Do you mean clouds in the sky?"

"Yes."

"A whole bunch," was my inspired answer. Finally I got a question I could sort of answer.

"Where was Jesus when He rose from the dead?" That's a fascinating question that I don't think the Bible answers completely. We know the tomb was empty on Easter Sunday morning, and we know He appeared to Mary that morning and later to the two disciples on the road to Emmaus. There were other appearances over the next forty days. But where was He during the time between those appearances? We don't really know. All we know is that sometime before dawn on Sunday morning, life returned to His dead body, He rose through His grave clothes, the stone was rolled away, and Jesus came out of the tomb, alive from the dead.

If you're asking where He was at 6:30 A.M. on Easter Sunday, my answer is, "I don't know where He was, but

I know where He wasn't. He wasn't in the tomb. Jesus had come back from the dead."

Life is hard for all of us, and we all have so many questions, doubts, fears, and worries. There are questions we cannot answer. So many people struggle with hurts and pains they can hardly express. Easter says to us, "The story isn't over yet." If you are a believer, history doesn't end with a question mark but with an exclamation point. As we've heard many times, "It's Friday, but Sunday's coming." This is the message of the Resurrection:

> Your doubts are not the end of the story.
> Your fears are not the end of the story.
> Your worries are not the end of the story.
> Your uncertainties are not the end of the story.
> Your unbelief is not the end of the story.

If we suffer with Him, we will reign with Him. *Because Jesus rose from the dead, better days are coming.* The grave will not have the last word. One day the children of God will exit the cemeteries once and for all. Let us be perfectly clear about it. We do believe that Jesus died and rose again; therefore we have no doubts that, one day, the dead in Christ will rise, and we will rise with them to meet the Lord in the air (1 Thessalonians 4:16–17). Between now and then, we are living on the edge, waiting for what God has promised. It's like a TV cliffhanger where the end of the episode says, "Come back next week to see how the story ends." Stay tuned, child of God. The best is yet to come.

And all of this, the certainty of eventual victory with our risen Lord, all of it goes back to the great purposes of God that stretch across the centuries, that span the ages, that reach from eternity past to eternity future. All of it goes back to the first truth that our God is absolutely sovereign and that our salvation rests not in our own puny strength but in the mighty hands of God whose purposes cannot fail.

If you believe that God has a plan for your life, then you can find the strength to keep on going. The sovereignty of God puts iron in a man. It makes him stand up straight for God. When a man understands this truth, it puts some *spizerinktum* in his soul. It's a wonderful thing when a man can say, "This is God's will, and I have found it. I've given my life to it."

A COMMAND WE NEED TO OBEY

"So then, brothers, stand firm and hold to the teachings we passed on to you, whether by word of mouth or by letter" (2 Thessalonians 2:15). The command in this verse flows directly from the doctrine of verses 13–14. If you understand the purposes of God, then you will have every motivation to do what Paul commands.

Stand firm! Hold on!

So many believers are jumpy, jittery, worried, and

uncertain. Who can blame them? If you watch too much news on TV, you're bound to get jittery sooner or later. Ever since 9/11/01, the newscasts have been filled with reports of terrorist attacks—some foiled, some successful. And every day brings news of more attacks and counterattacks. Truly, these are perilous times. No wonder so many people are on edge.

In times like these, we need to stand fast on the truth of God's sovereignty, and we need to hold on to the truth written down in the Word of God. What you know can save you when life tumbles in around you. When the ground seems unsteady under your feet, remember what you have learned. Go back to the first principles.

Lately I've been thinking a lot about a truth that is becoming more and more important to me. *Good theology can save your life.* In the time of trouble, if you know the truth and if you remember the truth, what you know and remember can save you from despair. On a radio program in Dallas, we took a call from a woman who was going through a hard time in her marriage, with her health, and with some family relationships. As I listened, I realized she was a Christian who felt overwhelmed. I knew I couldn't solve her problems in two minutes. So I told her that she needed to go back to the first principles and remind herself of those things she knew to be true. "Good theology can save your life," I told her. At that point the host broke in and said, "But you're a pastor. You have to say that." Yes, I am a pastor and I do have to say that, but I say it because it's true. What things are we talking about? Here's a short list of truth we can cling to at all times:

> God is good.
> God is faithful.
> He will never leave me.
> His mercy endures forever.
> This is no mistake.
> God has a purpose.
> He is working out His plan for me.
> God still loves me.
> The Holy Spirit indwells me.
> Jesus is alive today.
> He will return someday.

Sometimes all we can do is dig in and hold on. And when trouble comes, sometimes that's the best thing we can do. More than anything else, our generation of Christians needs to hear these words again: "Stand fast." Remember what you have learned. Stand on the truth you already know. Take God at His word! There is no reason to quit or to give in to evil.

A PRAYER WE NEED TO PRAY

"May our Lord Jesus Christ himself and God our Father, who loved us and by his grace gave us eternal

encouragement and good hope, encourage your hearts and strengthen you in every good deed and word" (2 Thessalonians 2:16–17). We come at last to the prayer of Paul for the Thessalonians. The context is crucial because the prayer flows directly from the doctrine of God's sovereignty and from the command to stand firm. First, we must remember that God is the source of all power. He alone can help us in the time of trouble. All the resources of heaven are at our disposal. Second, remember what God has already done for us. He has solved every problem by taking care of our past, our present, and our future.

> He loved us—that's in the past when He gave us His Son.
> He encouraged us—that's in the present through the ministry of the Holy Spirit.
> He gives us hope—that's in the future when we will share in His glory.

In light of all that, pray for two things:

> Pray for an encouraged heart.
> Pray for a stable heart.

When we are encouraged, we will face the trials of life with hope. As Charles Spurgeon said in one of his sermons, "Cheerfulness ought to be the atmosphere you breathe, and if you believe that God loves you, you cannot but be happy." When your heart is stabilized, you won't be swayed back and forth by circumstances and emotional mood swings. The latest headlines won't throw you for a loop one way or the other. The stable heart is fixed on the Lord and is not swaying to and fro. The mark of the stable heart is consistency. You are the same because Christ is the same no matter what happens around you.

And the result of the prayer is wonderful. You are able to do every good work and to say every good word the Lord wants you to do and to say. Your life and your lips are in harmony with the Lord.

Here's the passage in a nutshell: *Since God has chosen you for salvation, stand fast amid all the trials of life, knowing that God will encourage you and make you strong on the inside so that your life will be filled with good words and good deeds.* It's all there, and it all flows together—doctrine, command, and prayer. Here's another way of looking at it:

> You are greatly loved—Stand fast!
> You were chosen by God—Stand fast!
> You were called to salvation—Stand fast!
> You believed the gospel—Stand fast!
> You will one day share in Christ's glory—Stand fast!
> You have received God's comfort—Stand fast!

You have good hope by grace—Stand fast!
You were established in every word and deed—Stand
    fast!

You will be stable when Christ is in your heart. All that I have said about the doctrine, the command, and the prayer doesn't matter without Christ. Unless He is in your heart, the rest is just good religious advice. I often exhort unbelievers to "run to the cross!" But that's not just a good word for the lost. That's great advice for believers. In the time of trouble, run to Jesus. Cling to Him! Believe in Him! Trust in Him! Rest your soul in the Lord, and all will be well with your soul.

Heavenly Father, thank You for planning every detail of my life long before I was born. You alone are God, and there is no one like You. You reached out in love and drew me to the Savior. Thank You for including me in Your family. Now I pray to be made strong in all my weak places. Help me believe all You have said and to rest my life on Your promises. May I come to the end of my days still believing, still trusting, still hoping, still loving, and still serving You. Until the day comes when I see You face-to-face, make me strong so that I will not waver when hard times come. Lord Jesus, I gladly commit all that I have into Your hands, both now and forever.

Amen.

CONCLUSION

We have come to the end of our brief journey through the prayers of Paul. In the Introduction, I said that I hoped three things would happen as a result of studying the prayers of Paul in the New Testament:

1. We would know what Paul prayed for.
2. We would know what God is saying to us through the prayers of Paul.
3. We would know how to pray more effectively as a result.

In recent months I have found myself praying, "Lord, open the eyes of my heart that I might know You better." And I have asked God to strengthen others on the inside with power through the Spirit. And I prayed that my loved ones would have insight to make wise choices under pressure. These are themes that come directly from Paul's prayers. As we have seen, these first-century prayers speak directly to life in the twenty-first century.

LESSONS LEARNED

Among other things, Paul prayed for enlightenment, power, discernment, growth, love, encouragement, endurance, boldness, protection, and unity. He prayed for believers to be thankful, cheerful, strong, stable, and fruitful so that they would walk worthy of the Lord and bring great glory to God.

How can we summarize the prayers of Paul? Here is my own list. These prayers were:

1. Practical
2. Thankful
3. Fervent
4. Earnest
5. Regular
6. God-centered
7. Aimed at spiritual growth

8. Not focused on outward circumstances

9. Kingdom-centered

The following nine prayer themes sum up what Paul prayed for. They touch upon needs that we all have. Here is my challenge to you. Copy down the themes and place the list in your Bible, using it as a prayer guide this week. Or put it on your mirror so you have something to pray while you're getting ready in the morning. As you pray this week, pray along the lines of these nine points. Use them to pray for yourself, and use them as you pray for others.

Here are nine things we need based on the prayers of Paul:

Our first need is to know God better. This comes from Paul's prayer in Ephesians 1:15–23 where he prays that the eyes of your heart be opened to know God better. Until the Holy Spirit opens our eyes, we will never know God deeply and personally. This is where all spiritual growth must begin. Until we come to the knowledge of God, everything else is just religious decoration.

Our second need is a new appreciation of God's power to help us. In Ephesians 3, Paul prays that we might be strengthened with might through the Spirit in the inner man. This is a prayer for power on the inside so that we will be strong in the face of adversity.

Our third need is the ability to make wise choices

under pressure. When Paul wrote to the Philippians, he prayed that they might be filled with insight to choose those things that are best (Philippians 1:9–11). As we face many choices in life, we truly need God's help to sort out the good from the bad, the better from the good, and the best from the better. And we need the ability to do it on the spur of the moment and when the pressure is on, which is where most of life's decisions are made.

Our fourth need is genuine love for others. This theme comes up again and again in Paul's prayers. In Philippians 1:9, he prays that their love may increase and abound toward each other. Overflowing love is made visible in the way we treat other people. It is one of the most obvious proofs that we know Jesus Christ.

Our fifth need is strength to endure so we won't give up. In Colossians 1:11, Paul prays for strength that leads to patience and endurance. We need this for those inevitable times when the going is rough, when things aren't going our way, when it would be easy to give up, and when we are tempted to throw in the towel, and say, "I quit!"

Our sixth need is a willingness to trust God for the impossible. At the end of his prayer in Ephesians 3, Paul offers this doxology: **"Now to him who is able to do immeasurably more than all we ask or imagine, according to his power that is at work within us"** (v. 20). God's power is far beyond our imagination. Our largest, boldest prayers don't begin to exhaust his mighty power. We need strong faith in a big God to overcome the challenges we face.

Our seventh need is a life pleasing to the Lord Jesus Christ. In Colossians 1:10 Paul prays that his readers would walk worthy of the Lord. This means living in such a way that God is pleased with us. This touches every part of life, from the tiniest choices to the most major decisions.

Our eighth need is growing thankfulness to God. Paul's prayer in Colossians 1 ends with a call for thanksgiving based on all the blessings of God in salvation. This includes redemption, becoming citizens of God's kingdom, and having a great inheritance in the life to come. We ought to be thankful when we consider all that God has done for us—past, present, and future.

Our ninth need is cheerfulness in the midst of our trials. In 2 Thessalonians 2:17, Paul prayed that the believers might have encouragement and strength as they endured persecution. Likewise, we should pray for a "heavenly perspective" during our trials so that we can have joy even during the hardest moments.

A Final Reminder

Let us pray like Paul every day. And then let's stand back and see what God will do.

Great doors are open before us—Pray!

Great challenges face us—Pray!
Great needs rise in our path—Pray!

All things are possible when the church begins to pray. So, Lord, do whatever it takes, but please, O Lord, teach us to pray. Amen.

Notes

Chapter 1: Don't Settle for Second Best

1. *Marvin's Room,* adapted by Scott McPherson from his 1990 stage play, prod. Scott Rudin, dir. Jerry Zaks, 1 hr. 38 min., Miramax Films, 1996, videocassette.

Chapter 2: How to Pray with Power

1. John Eldredge, *Wild at Heart* (Thomas Nelson: Nashville, 2001).

Chapter 3: Open My Eyes, Lord

1. "Sweet Hour of Prayer," William W. Walford, 1772–1850, public domain.

Chapter 4: Beyond Your Dreams

1. John MacArthur, *Ephesians* (Chicago: Moody, 1986), 103–4.

2. Sermon by W. A. Criswell, *Love for the Lost World,* December 5, 1976, http://www.wacriswell.org/index.cfm/FuseAction/Search.Transcripts/ sermon/2197.cfm.

3. John Stott, *God's New Society: The Message of Ephesians* (Downers Grove: InterVarsity, 1979), 139–40.

Chapter 5: Hanging Tough for Jesus

1. Story from http://www.worthynews.com/christian-persecution/features/ muslim-extremist-murders.html.

Chapter 6: Strength for the Journey

1. Pat Williams, *How to Be Like Jesus: Lessons on Following in His Footsteps,* (Faith Communications: Deerfield Beach, Fla.), 237, 250–52.

Conclusion

1. Edgar A. Guest, *Sermons We See.* Guest (1881–1959) began his illustrious career in 1895 at the age of fourteen when his work first appeared in the *Detroit Free Press.* His column was syndicated in over 300 newspapers, and he became known as "The Poet of the People."

If you would like to contact the author, you can reach him in the following ways:

By letter:
Ray Pritchard
Calvary Memorial Church
931 Lake Street
Oak Park, IL 60301

By e-mail: PastorRay@calvarymemorial.com

Via the Internet: www.calvarymemorial.com

An Anchor for the Soul Series

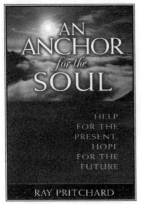

ISBN: 0-8024-1535-0

Anchor for the Soul

An Anchor for the Soul is a straight-forward, easily readable book — the perfect introduction for those just beginning their Christian journey, or for those considering new steps toward God.

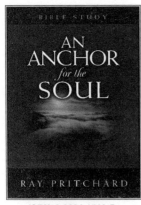

ISBN: 0-8024-1510-5

Anchor for the Soul Bible Study

Have you ever wondered . . .
> *What is God like?*
> *How can we really know Him?*

Ray Pritchard reveals the answers to these honest and important questions through the good news of the gospel. It is possible to know God deeply and personally. All you have to do is have the desire to know Him, and, by knowing God, you can experience His power in your life.

MOODY
PUBLISHERS
THE NAME YOU CAN TRUST.

1-800-678-6928 www.MoodyPublishers.org

SINCE 1894, Moody Publishers has been dedicated to equip and motivate people to advance the cause of Christ by publishing evangelical Christian literature and other media for all ages, around the world. Because we are a ministry of the Moody Bible Institute of Chicago, a portion of the proceeds from the sale of this book go to train the next generation of Christian leaders.

If we may serve you in any way in your spiritual journey toward understanding Christ and the Christian life, please contact us at www.moodypublishers.com.

"All Scripture is God-breathed and is useful for teaching, rebuking, correcting and training in righteousness, so that the man of God may be thoroughly equipped for every good work."
—*2 TIMOTHY 3:16, 17*

MOODY
PUBLISHERS

THE NAME YOU CAN TRUST®

BEYOND ALL YOU COULD ASK OR THINK TEAM

ACQUIRING EDITOR
Greg Thornton

COPY EDITOR
Ali Childers

BACK COVER COPY
Anne Perdicaris

COVER DESIGN
Paetzold Associates

COVER PHOTO
Pat Powers and Cherryl Schafer/Photodisc

INTERIOR DESIGN
Ragont Design

PRINTING AND BINDING
Quebecor World Book Services

The typeface for the text of this book is
Agaramond